Legends of the
BAGGY
GREEN

Legends of the
BAGGY
GREEN

Dubious behaviour & achievements from cricket's
chequered history

ALEXANDER BUZO

ALLEN&UNWIN

Allen & Unwin
83 Alexander Street
Crows Nest NSW 2065
Australia
Phone: (61 2) 8425 0100
Fax: (61 2) 9906 2218
Email: info@allenandunwin.com
Web: www.allenandunwin.com

National Library of Australia
Cataloguing-in-Publication entry:

Buzo, Alexander, 1944- .
    Legends of the baggy green : dubious behaviour and
    achievements from cricket's chequered history.

    ISBN 1 74114 385 3.

    1. Cricket - Corrupt practices. 2. Cricket - Rules -
    History. 3. Cricket - Australia. 4. Test matches
    (Cricket). I. Title.

796.358

Set in 12/17 pt Bembo by Bookhouse, Sydney
Printed by McPherson's Printing Group, Maryborough

10 9 8 7 6 5 4 3 2 1

Contents

To John and Kay Ward, with thanks.

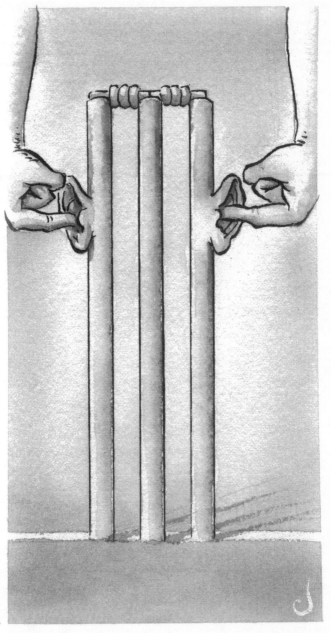

JOCK ALEXANDER

1

Oo-wah!

It was the fourth day of the fourth test in Antigua on a windy May day in 2003 and Ramnaresh Sarwan was heading for his first century against Australia. Hoping to focus his thoughts on other topics, bowler Glenn McGrath greeted him at the non-striker's end with an enquiry: 'What does Brian Lara's cock taste like?'

The beanpole quick then waited for an answer.

Sarwan, loyal to his leader, responded: 'I don't know, ask your wife.'

As an attempt to introduce a more savoury note into the conversation, this was a failure.

'If you ever fuckin' mention my wife again, I'll fuckin' cut your throat out,' shouted McGrath, towering over the Indian-descended Sarwan and pointing for emphasis.

Then followed a complaint about sledging to the umpire . . . by McGrath.

As a watershed in modern cricket behaviour, this had a lot going for it. The images flashed around the world, lip-readers had their day in the sun, sports page moralists fumed, and boards of control had themselves a ready-made item one. All eyes turned to the match referee, and what did the match referee do? Nothing.

The 1995 image of the Caribbean tour, of the giant black African-descended Curtly Ambrose menacing the compact figure of Steve Waugh, was replaced by the tiny Sarwan being monstered by the bullying imperialist white bowler, who had been christened 'Oo-ah Glenn McGrath' by Anne Fulwood and other adoring women. McGrath's wife had been undergoing treatment for cancer, but Sarwan was not thinking about this—if he knew—when he uttered his famous six little words. The two players were bound together in the tableau by anger and anguish in roughly equal amounts.

The inaction by the match referee triggered even more controversy, and that most inescapable of modern prunes, the politically correct rugger-bugger, had a field month, churning out articles and comments condemning McGrath and finding Sarwan blameless. Nothing, it seems, will stop white men from attacking other white men. The *Sydney Morning Herald* went further than most, naming McGrath as 'the biggest prat of 2003'. (For the benefit of readers younger than the *SMH* sports section attracts, there was an old joke about the difference between a cowboy and a prostitute: one has a prairie hat and the other a hairy prat.)

Only one person defended the actions of the big quick: Jane McGrath, whom no one thought to ask in the immediate aftermath. Just over a year later, on 31 May 2004, she described her response on the ABC's *Enough Rope*, saying to her husband, 'Thank you for defending me and standing up for me and that is the way I would hope any man that loved his wife or partner or child would react.'

What happened back at the cricket on the following day, 12 May 2003? Sarwan got his century and the West Indies went on to a historic victory, scoring a record 7 for 418 in the fourth innings. That was all.

The other result? The 'sledge pledge' on better behaviour and all that and all this . . . this being a book of commentary, hopefully reasonably objective, on the manners, mores, controversies, quirks and scandals of the summer game, is told, I hope, with the amount of humour and lyricism this perverse sport demands.

ARTHUR MAILEY

H. L. Collins

'It was no wonder that when the massive Warwick Armstrong shambled out of cricket after the 1921 tour, the "Little Corporal" should take his place.'

2

It's a stew

Collins is just as often missed, parlez-vous
As mademoiselle has ever been kissed, parlez-vous
It's good safe betting to put your shirt
On Fortune's odds-on favourite Bert
Inky-pinky parlez-vous.

1921 Australian team song

The domestic life of Salim Malik; do we want to go there?

Called 'Solemn Alec' by one commentator, and 'the Rat' by several players, Malik (the name actually means 'man of steel') founded the modern era of cricket scandal when he approached Tim May and Shane Warne and asked them to bowl badly and 'throw' the first test in Pakistan in 1994. The spinners refused, and Australia lost by one wicket in a thriller, when Ian Healy missed stumping Inzamam off Warne and the ball went for four byes.

'Why do you call him the Rat?' Warne was asked by an interviewer.

'Because he looks like one,' replied the unpretentious bowler.

Home life with Salim Malik would undoubtedly be tranquil for the most part, and there is no reason to believe otherwise—except when cricket is on television. It is easy to imagine the scene: Mrs Malik in an armchair, a few sprogs lounging on the sofa, some good friends sipping Diet Sprite, a delicious Peshwari nan on the coffee table, everyone enjoying the live telecast, and then Salim walks in. 'Don't tell me the result!' they all chorus.

Malik was not punished for his role in match-fixing for some time afterwards, being a valuable and high-scoring batsman for Pakistan. He continued to play, and when he walked out to bat in Melbourne a spectator shouted: 'The cheque's in the mail.'

Spoonerisms are heard on television from time to time, such as when Slack's Creek, Brisbane, was in the news, and Sky Television's Garry Wilkinson announced 'A fire has broken out in Sleek Cracks.' Dear me, Wilko! What were you thinking of? Such was the degree to which match-fixing was in the air around the early 2000s that a simple spoonerism in the commercial for a game on Fox Sports sounded ominous rather than quirky: 'Be watching tomorrow live at 7.00 p.m. when England beat Pakistan in one-day international cricket at Edgmaston.' Obviously the teams were going to *meet* at *Edgbaston*, but in the climate of 'fatch-mixing' even the most innocent mistake had sinister overtones.

Dyslexia is a harmless and common affliction and dyslexics live a normal life—although screenwriter Jacques Prevert was never keen to have them in the graphics department—and so do the users of clichés such as 'a promoter's dream', but all of a sudden there were clouds of suspicion everywhere. India lost the Boxing Day test in Melbourne in 2003, squaring the series, and a simple news report that 'the nine-wicket loss has turned the New Year Sydney test into a promoter's dream' made it sound like a case for Inspector Morse. Did they say the Year of the Rat? It was the Decade of the Rat.

On the face of it, McGrath and Malik are the founding fathers of modern controversy and scandal, but alas, all was not rosy in the supposed Garden of Eden that was cricket in the 'olden days'.

There are two kinds of match-fixing: losing or drawing to bump up the gate for a decider so everyone benefits, and the sinister, subcontinental organised crime fix. One is a straightforward example of the manly art of deception, a financial arm ball, and the other a devious, despicable end-of-civilisation piece of chicanery devised by black-eyed Souzas in the smoke-filled dens of Kolkata and Karachi.

'Bradman Denies Fourth Test Rigged' boomed the headline on Sydney's *Daily Mirror*, 6 February 1963. The crux of the story was reported thus:

> Sir Donald was angered by a correspondent who alleged in a letter to the *Adelaide News* that Richie Benaud had been under orders from the Board of Control to 'play for the gates' in the fourth test in Adelaide.

Draws were not an unlikely outcome on the batsman's paradise that is Adelaide Oval, but the upshot was that the 1962–63 Ashes series went to the fifth and final test in Sydney at one-all. Whenever this happens, in pubs all over Australia, the cry goes up: 'It's a stew.' It happened in 1974–75 when the third test in Melbourne was drawn and the series went to Sydney with the Ashes still undecided and a big crowd was attracted. It happens whenever a three-match one-day finals series is levelled at one-all.

Journalist David Thorpe was unwise enough to put pub talk into print in 1982 when he suggested that the West Indies had 'played for the gates' in a one-day series. Under a headline in the *Age*, 'Come On, Dollar, Come On', Thorpe alleged that the West Indies had thrown a game against Australia so the home side would go ahead of Pakistan and make the finals, thus ensuring a bigger gate than a West Indies–Pakistan final. He was successfully sued by Windies skipper Clive Lloyd in an historic case—the last time an appeal went to the Privy Council in London.

In other sports it is common for allegations of match-fixing to be made. The Sydney rugby league grand finals of 1952 and 1963 were regarded by Resch's philosophers as 'stews' that had been cooked up by referees George Bishop and Darcy Lawler respectively, in association with bookmakers. Sir Donald Bradman regarded cricket as immune from this kind of temptation:

> Your correspondent would do a finer service to mankind if he stopped such baseless accusations and accepted the fact that in cricket the leaders are imbued with a spirit of honesty and integrity which will be steadfastly maintained at all times.
>
> Yours faithfully,
> Don Bradman

In his cricketing autobiography *10 for 66 and All That*, Arthur Mailey relates a rather different incident from the Adelaide test in 1924–25. The first revelation—shocking to the teenager that I was when I first read it—was that sportsmen stayed up all night. Mailey, Johnny Taylor and skipper Bert Collins were renting a flat near the Adelaide Oval, and on the eve of the last day of the test, they 'put on gramophone records and had supper in the middle of which dawn broke'. The day's play ahead of them would not be a full one—England needed only 27 to win with two wickets in hand—but just the same, to someone brought up on the unchallenged philosophy of 'nine hours sleep and a steak at 10.00 a.m.' as the ideal athlete's preparation, this was pretty racy stuff. It got racier.

Before the red-eyed trio left for the ground, Collins was approached in the hall by a 'fabulous-looking race-course man'. After a few moments of conversation, the Australian captain came over to Mailey and said: 'This fellow says it's worth a hundred quid if we lose the match. Let's throw him downstairs.' The racecourse man apparently overheard this and disappeared. Was Collins upset at the implication that he was bribable, or did he think a hundred pounds was an insultingly low offer?

Mailey, a great defender of the man he called 'Mauldy', insists that Collins 'gambled anywhere except on the cricket field, and on anything but cricket'. England lost the test by eleven runs, and with it the series, with two tests still to go; there was no 'playing for the gates' in Adelaide on this trip. The City of Churches, where people have names like Clayvel Badcock and Tarlton Jefferis, and suburbs are called St John's Wood, retained its aura of respectability this time.

Australia had bounced back from World War I much quicker than England, winning the first three series in 1920–21, 1921 and 1924–25. In 1926, eight years after the war ended, England won back the Ashes, just as they did eight years after World War II, after losing in 1946–47, 1948, 1950–51, then winning the fifth and deciding test in 1953 after four draws. The patterns of history suggest an ultimately successful postwar reconstruction effort on England's part, but then along came 'Stork'.

Hunter Hendry may have an Adelaide-sounding name, but this tall, thin former Australian test cricket captain comes from Sydney and ended up in Melbourne. Nicknamed Stork after being spotted standing on one leg in the slips, he alleged in a 1988 interview that Herbert 'Horseshoe' Collins, as Australian captain, 'threw' the deciding Oval test in 1926 by bowling a second-rank off-spinner, Arthur Richardson, to a packed leg-side field, and thus allowing England off the hook. It was a sticky wicket and fast bowler Jack Gregory would have been unplayable, experts thought, although one newspaper reported Gregory as nursing a shin injury. ('Fast bowler' here is a relative term, for in 1926 Arne Borg won the 1500 metres freestyle at the European swimming championships in 21 minutes 29 seconds, almost exactly 50 per cent slower than Grant Hackett in the modern era.)

Having decided to go with slow bowlers, 'Lucky' Collins set his field deep when both batsmen were popping the ball up at catchable height. It is only fair to record that many observers rated England the better team (they went on to thrash Australia 4–1 in 1928–29) and others thought the Australians were jaded after the exhausting itinerary ('if it's Thursday this must be Somerset') the MCC thoughtfully drew up for them. Collins was recovering from neuritis, and after four draws it was agreed that the fifth test would be played to a finish. It certainly finished Collins; the Little Corporal never played in another test, or indeed any first-class cricket, ever again.

Hendry was interviewed by Paul Brown for a cricket magazine, but his allegations of match-fixing were not published until 2000 in a *Sydney Morning Herald* article by Spiro Zavos. This was the crucial passage:

BROWN: What was Herbie Collins like?

HENDRY: Oh, I disregard him altogether. Oh, I wouldn't have him at all.

BROWN: I thought that Collins was supposed to be a very shrewd captain.

HENDRY: He was supposed to be an astute and shrewd captain, but if I told you that he sold a test match, a deciding test match in England, you would hardly believe me, but he did!

BROWN: Oh, really?

HENDRY: Yes. It was in 1926. I had scarlet fever, unfortunately, and was seven weeks in hospital but I came out to watch the last test match at The Oval. A proper sticky wicket we had England on and he [Collins] had Arthur

Richardson bowling off-breaks on the leg stump to a leg field! Now ask yourself, anybody with the slightest common sense would know bloody well that that must have been a sell-out. Well, of course, he was a . . . I do not know if you know his background, but he was always in financial trouble. He was an SP bookmaker and this and that and the other thing . . . I always thought he was over-rated as a captain.

Was Herby Collins guilty? Was he the biggest prat of 1926? Is this where bad behaviour began? Or was it, as Roy Orbison would later ask, too soon to know?

When the fourth test of this series finished in Manchester the Australians were put on a 10.00 p.m. train which arrived in London at 6.00 a.m., a schedule which had the fingerprints of MCC chairman Lord Harris's fine Italian hand all over it. Nevertheless, there was little sympathy from the Australian press. Writing in *The Referee*, 'Not Out' (they all had names like that) opined: 'It would have been tragical if the 1926 team had beaten England in England.' In the light of Hunter Hendry's bombshell, another observation on the Oval showdown in *The Referee* takes on more sinister overtones: 'The Australians were playing as though they wanted to get it over quickly.' As for the deep-set field when the ball was popping, 'Sutcliffe was enjoying uncanny immunity from danger in making such shots.'

Herbert Sutcliffe and Jack Hobbs put on an opening stand of 172 in England's second innings, largely off Richardson's bowling, and this is where the match was won. Sutcliffe went on to make 161 before being skittled by a Mailey wrong 'un, and then Australia collapsed in the final innings, with Mailey being the last man out and the souvenirer of the ball. Hobbs was later interviewed by 'The Australian Press Association, London, August 19' (they all had bylines like that) for the *Sydney Morning Herald*, saying, 'Richardson's bowling was excellent, but it was negative. He seemed not to be trying for a wicket, but rather was waiting for the batsmen to get themselves out.' Hobbs finished up with a tribute to his opponents: 'I cannot pay sufficient tribute to their generosity. One of the pleasantest of all my cricket recollections will be Collins's handshake as I completed my century.' Hmm. The shadow of the Hendry interview certainly falls across that little quote.

If 'Cricket is a series of individual confrontations disguised as a team game' (Peter Roebuck), then the duel between Richardson and Sutcliffe was the main event, with Sutcliffe feeling he had been savaged by a dead sheep and that England had taken a winning position. Many years later, in 1998, the discredited South African captain Hansie Cronje directed off-spinner Pat Symcox to 'do a Richardson' and bowl on the leg stump to a packed on-side field in the Sydney test. Australian ex-player and commentator Ashley Mallett thought Cronje was deliberately thowing away a strong position and faxed his thoughts to Ali Bacher, CEO of the United Cricket Board of South Africa. Mallett was perhaps ahead of his time, as it was not until 2000 that the full extent of the South African shenanigans became known, and Cronje was banned for life.

The defence—that they only threw a few 'meaningless' one-day internationals—showed that cricket had not fully adjusted to its position in the world of professional entertainment. If tickets are sold and people turn up to watch, then it is not 'meaningless'. Broadway musicals are performed eight times a week as long as there is a paying audience; you do not find actors 'throwing' a 'meaningless' matinee. In professional entertainment the box office *is* the 'meaning'.

Stork Hendry alleged that Herby Collins lost the Oval test in 1926 by arrangement with London bookmakers, in order to pay off his gambling debts. An addicted gambler who later became a bookmaker, Collins was a heavy loser and in 1931 he applied to the NSW Cricket Association for financial relief. Hendry is the only person to have made these charges against Collins, and Hendry is of course an honourable man, but there is no hard evidence and certainly no proof. To the accusation that Gregory would have been a better choice as bowler than Richardson, Collins could, if called upon to defend himself, point out that Gregory had only taken one wicket in the series and that poor embattled Richo—in the innings in question—claimed two important scalps, Frank Woolley and skipper Percy Chapman, who were both specialist batsmen. He might also point out that England won by 289 runs, so it was fairly emphatic all round, and that the good Stork had a test average of only 20.94 and had not played in the previous series (1924–25) when Collins had been captain and an influence with selectors. Did Hendry have a grudge? Or the chip that comes with a low average? Arthur Mailey worshipped the Little Corporal and Mailey is an honourable man.

Proving bad behaviour—it's a bitch.

Things were different towards the end of the twentieth century, when Salim Malik was tried, convicted of match-fixing and banned from cricket for life—admittedly when he was well past his best. Questionable behaviour has always been a part of cricket, but it is more difficult now to hide it from the eyes of the prying scribes. Monty Noble was said to have been verbally critical of 'Lucky' Collins and Arthur Richardson in the press box at the Oval in 1926, but he told his 'ghost' not to write down what he said, so it would not 'hurt anyone's feelings'. Legendary sportswriter Tom Goodman always praised and never knocked, so much so that he was made a life member of the New South Wales Rugby League. The journalist who broke the Salim Malik story in

1995—albeit in terms that had to be 'legalled' (i.e. not mentioning Malik by name after legal advice)—was Phil Wilkins, who described his approach to the scoop five years later:

> Every good journo has his day. Every decent workaholic has one great story in his deadline-ulcered, family-ruptured, wine-sodden life when he knows he has stumbled on to a world exclusive.

What was the response of his target? Were the accused's feelings hurt?

'I'll sue you, Pheel,' said Solemn Alec.

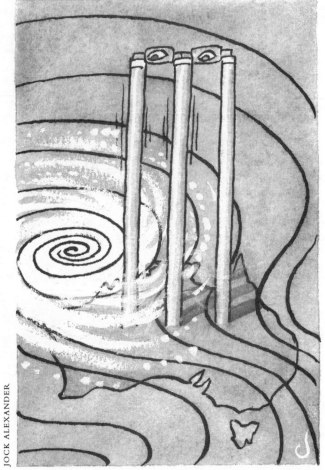

3

Civilising global cricket

It's not a garden party, you know.

Reg 'Toecutter' Withers

Oooh! He stuck his tongue in!

Madge Cruickshank

English players on the Bodyline tour of 1932–33 were ritually excoriated for prostituting the noble game, for unethical behaviour, for violating the spirit of cricket and for all-round bastardry. Their aim—to beat Australia by curbing Don Bradman, using fair means or foul—had been realised in spades, but month after month, year after year, they were trotted out as the villains of world cricket. Eventually, one of them—believed to have been Bill

Voce—snapped to a pious journalist, 'You didn't think we were going to go all that way just to give that little fellow some batting practice, did you?'

An unwieldy sport that lays itself open to all kinds of abuse, cricket has always moved against bad behaviour on two fronts: voluntary codes and changes to the rules. As a result of the Bodyline tour there were private pledges not to bowl at the batsman's body, and the rules were changed to allow only two fielders behind square leg. The days of 'leg theory', of Larwood and Voce hurling their thunderbolts rib-high to a packed leg-side field waiting to snaffle the fended off scraps, were over by the start of the 1934 Ashes series. Once again, Australia triumphed and 'the Don' got plenty of batting practice.

The Australian bowling attack was led by Bill O'Reilly, a leg-spinner who continued in the tradition of Arthur Mailey and Clarrie Grimmett, taking heaps of English wickets and finding a niche beside them in the record books. England specialised in off-spin and in 1937 they persuaded Australia to accept another rule change: a batsman could be out leg before wicket to a ball pitching outside off stump, but not to a ball pitching outside leg stump. Bill O'Reilly fumed for years, pointing out how unfair this was to leggies and the hard, bouncy pitches of the Antipodes, and how biased in favour of finger-spinners operating on the soft green turf of the Old Dart, but there was little he could do. He would have—almost certainly—taken some satisfaction from Bradman's last test innings. The Don was bowled for a duck by a wrong 'un from Eric Hollies, one of very few English wrist-spinners and the third last one to play for England (Doug Wright and Tommy Greenhough essentially performed the last rites for English leg-spin in the 1950s, and brief appearances by Hobbs and then Salisbury and Schofield in the 1990s confirmed this).

The political equivalent of the Bodyline tour was the dismissal of the Whitlam government in 1975 after a Labor senator died and was replaced by a stooge who voted for the opposition. Liberal senate leader Reg Withers wore the charges of unethical behaviour, of returning to office via a dead delivery boy, of prostituting the spirit of democracy and so on, for years, until he, too, finally snapped when questioned by a pious journalist. 'Politics is about gaining power. It's not a garden party, you know,' revealed the man they called 'the Toecutter'.

In politics, as in cricket, we are dealing, after all, with, er, human nature.

Officially, a batsman is not out until the umpire says so, but in England the practice of 'walking' became institutionalised. If a batsman got an edge and was caught by the keeper he did not wait for the umpire, he walked. It looked good, it looked sporting, and if he didn't do it the umpire would pass his name around the other county umpires and that batsman would be out to any and all lbw (or 'leg before wicket' for the acronym-phobic) appeals in future knocks. As in so many aspects of the summer game, the working model is ethics by persuasion.

In Australia, as the shockingly jocular English commentators say, cricketers only walk if their car breaks down. Even if they get a thick edge to the keeper, batsmen will stand their ground, sometimes rubbing an arm, and wait for the umpire's decision. Their reasoning is that the good and bad decisions even out over a season, and if they escape the noose this time, it makes up for the bad decision last time. For 'the shoc-joc' English commentator, this is evidence of a convict sense of injustice, of not giving yourself up to the redcoats.

Of course, not all Englishmen walked all the time; when Henry Jupp, who played in the first test series against Australia in 1877, was out in a match at Dorking he did not budge from the crease.

'Aren't you walking?' inquired the keeper.

'Not at Dorking,' said Juppy. W.G. and E.M. Grace harboured similar thoughts about walking in remote areas and were even known to replace the bails after being bowled. 'Grace Brothers removals' became more difficult to effect the further from London the bearded duo played. Eric Hollies, it should be noted, always walked in county matches, and as a result had a higher batting average in test cricket (5.28) than in his first-class career (5.01). Hollers took 2323 wickets overall, which equals the number of times Ian Chappell has mentioned the Victor Richardson Gates at Adelaide Oval.

What is the system in South Africa? According to former test player John Traicos, the English practice of walking was entrenched until they played Australia in three series between 1963 and 1970. Realising they were at a disadvantage if they walked, the South Africans stood their ground and the Australian system was adopted right across the country.

'In 2002,' said Simon Taufel on *Inside Cricket*, 'umpires in test cricket got it right 88 per cent of the time. We'd like to see it closer to 95 per cent, but 88 is still pretty good.' Taufs is himself a respected test umpire, and he is being realistic. Until the computerised Hawk-Eye gets involved and umpiring decisions are right 100 per cent of the time, we are not going to see walking adopted as a voluntary code, custom, practice or rule. It is also salutary to remember the words of Cliff, the umpire in a play written by a former first-class captain: 'I was always a bowler's man. It's a tough game for bowlers, and I tried to help them as best I could.'

Who would walk for Cliff in the event of a reprieve? And is Cliff right? If a batsman snicks the ball on to his stumps he is out bowled, and if the ball hits his pad in front he is out lbw. Why, then, if he snicks it on to his pad, and it would have hit the stumps, is he not out? It is indeed a tough game for bowlers.

'Every match from second grade up is basically a shit-fight,' said another umpire, Geoff Denyer, when I asked him about player behaviour. With so much money at stake and so much competition for places in every team from second grade up, umpires are struggling to keep order among the appeal-crazy hordes, much less encourage good behaviour, and would probably faint if a batsman walked. People who profess to be shocked at the standard of modern sportsmanship tend to be flighty types like the film actress Madge Cruickshank on the *D Generation*. She suddenly broke up a love scene and ruined the take by spitting and fuming and wailing and complaining, 'He stuck his tongue in.' Oh dear. In the real world, Madge, tongues happen.

Some codes of conduct operate purely among players and are usually related to selfish behaviour. The head-master at my school was a rugby man who was proud of the Wallabies we had produced, but not all that keen on cricket. Rugby, he believed, was a team game that had educational value, whereas cricket . . . 'It's called a team game, but I'm not so sure,' he said, echoing the Roebuck line about individual confrontation. 'There isn't the same degree of leadership or pressure or cooperation.'

Both sports were compulsory and were expected to produce 'team players', but not much hope was held out for mere cricketers, those selfish and introverted waifs, and the Armidale School has not produced a single first-class player since it opened its gates in 1894.

Finding team spirit—it's a tough one. 'I have never known a player to be so loved by the public, yet discarded by his fellow players,' said Hunter Hendry of Don Bradman. 'Don simply sucked the orange dry. If you batted with him, there was no way you would get the strike.' Stork's views are quite common among those who played with the Don. The idolising of Bradman, or Bradolatry for short, has increased dramatically since his death in 2001, but his 'team-mates' have not joined in the celebrations with much enthusiasm.

More modern paradigms of selfishness would have to be headed by Geoff (or Geoffrey, as he prefers) Boycott. In his autobiography, Ian Botham writes: 'Carrying out the order of vice-captain Willis to run out skipper Boycott did more for my standing within the English camp than any runs or wickets.' It could be argued that this incident showed a high degree of leadership, cooperation and team spirit, except that it did not involve the leader. This is of course not the only story to deal with Boycott and his attitude to team spirit.

When Jack Egan was on a private tour of India he heard that on his last visit the resolute Yorkshireman was the only England player to read a new Indian spinner. Wickets fell all around him and he looked like being stranded. After playing and missing several times, a tailender asked Boycott how to deal with this mystery bowler. 'Just play him like an off-spinner,' advised Boycs, 'but don't tell any of the other fellows.'

Modern commentators are fond of 'killer stats' and one of them came up with the bizarre information that Steve Waugh had been involved in 27 run outs in his test career, and in 23 of them his partner was the one to go. Was this an indication of selfishness? It could have been the good luck that every cricketer needs, for Steve Waugh is an honourable man and Australian of the Year. His record number of 'not outs' (46 in 168 tests) was also aired when his farewell season ended in 2004. Did he leave rabbits to fend for themselves instead of farming the strike or going the tonk? His test average of 51.06 would have been reduced to 42.02 if the not outs had been outs, and 50 is what separates the goods from the greats.

In the first test against India at Brisbane in 2003, Waugh crossed with the outgoing batsman, centurion Justin Langer, thus ruining the ovation that was being accorded to the little opener. Waugh dismissed this idea at a press conference saying, 'He'd already had two standing ovies.' The fact that he crossed with his team-mate, and crossed at all costs, is to be applauded, especially by those with a sense of perspective.

In the 1950s, as Bob Simpson has revealed, the attitude of the players to the fans was 'Let the public and the cricket take care of themselves.' It was Richie Benaud in

1958 who introduced, as an inflexible team rule, the idea of the incoming batsmen and the outgoing batsman crossing on the field at the fall of a wicket, so the spectators didn't experience a hiatus in their day's entertainment. It was not a tactic to unsettle the opposition or cut down on their rest time; it was designed to keep the customers happy.

This was the first recognition of the public by any captain—indeed, any cricketer—and the first private rule or code that took into account the idea that professional sport is part of show business. It was the *only* such recognition, but it was a start, and presaged Benaud's involvement with the showbiz-oriented World Series Cricket almost twenty years later. It was also a companion piece to the rule/law/code/suggestion adopted by New South Wales Rugby League at the same time, that the player who scores a try then walks back and hands the ball to the goal-kicker so that the spectators can get a good look at his number and know who scored.

When this was first adopted there were lots of sheepish grins and satirical head-shakes on the part of the players, who rightly divined that they were taking part in a piece of play-acting. Some even made a big show of 'forgetting' and running back to scoop up the ball with a bow from the waist and then handing it to the kicker as if to say 'This wasn't my idea' or 'I'm not a show pony', but as the 1960s dawned it gradually sank in that those people who paid at the turnstiles were paying the players' wages and the shiny new Vauxhall Velox out in the parking lot was bought with last year's football earnings.

As the showbiz elements in professional sport increased (ground announcers were introduced to cricket in the late 1970s; before then, spectators had to bloody well work things out for themselves), so did the rise of agents and managers for the players, so much so that coach John Buchanan blamed the ten per centers for Australia's loss to India in the second test at Adelaide in 2003. Instead of working out tactics and building up mentally for an innings, these cricketers, representing their country, had been comparing their fees for sunglasses commercials. Since the days of Grant Kenny and his long relationship with Uncle Toby ('cereal monogamy', as Kathy Lette would say), the contracts had got shorter and the money more competitive, so the boys were doing comparisons when they should have been cleaning their spikes.

Back in the amateur days of rugby, television commentator Gordon Bray had been famous for his rampant CVs, whereby he would introduce biographic material at the most unlikely times ('He's in for a try! He's doing a PhD on the reproductive cycle of the ewe!'). It did not become inconceivable that a cricket commentator of the modern era could 'bray' at a vital moment: 'And he reaches his century! He's just signed with Kellogg's and made a profit on his Gold Coast unit!'

Buchanan did not like these trends and he was also concerned that the money men had too much control over the players' lives and careers ('My manager will give you my birthdate'), to the detriment of their cricket and powers of concentration. 'Buck' introduced a voluntary code, whereby players did not discuss sponsorship deals in the dressing room, much less in the slips, and this was promptly denounced by leading agent Sam Halvorsen, who is seen by some as Australia's Jerry Maguire.

The Tom Cruise film *Jerry Maguire* is not, as the inattentive still think, a bio-pic about an IRA operative who plants bombs in Belfast. The film in fact highlighted the growing power and indispensability of the sports agent in an age when actors and athletes are finding their roles colliding. Jerry introduces a code of ethics, a 'mission statement', to his firm and is promptly fired ('Ve don't do ethical here!'). He sets up an independent sports agency with his secretary (played by Renee Zellweger), but only one of his previous clients, a footballer called Rod Tidwell (played by Cuba Gooding Jr), stays with him, under the one condition: 'Show me the money.' This quickly became a catchphrase among multi-millionaire sports stars represented by powerful agencies, and Jerry Maguire's plea for integrity and independence became somewhat lost. Jerry eventually triumphs, gets the girl, and continues as a sports agent, but the message many would take from the film is 'Don't step out of line with the powers that be.' The late Victorian coach David Hookes's irreverent statement—'I never became an administrator because I don't have a blue blazer and dandruff'—was definitely Not the Way to Go.

Ian Chappell is a traditionalist in many ways, as befits the grandson of former test captain Vic Richardson, and he thought the last good coach was made by Cobb and Co. He did *not* think any team needed to be coached, much less the Australian test side. 'Chaps' was therefore no ally to John Buchanan, the man most people called a genius or a guru, but whom Mark Ray suggested might prove to be 'an accident-prone five-cent philosopher'. Buck had coached Queensland to its first Sheffield Shield victory and presided over an Australian team that was as far ahead of the other countries as the West Indies had been in the 1980s, but he was said to be too fond of quoting obscure Chinese warrior theorists, too tactless about bowlers' waistlines at press conferences, and had seen the position of coach lose all selection powers. One code he broke—albeit through a leaked letter to the players complaining about the influence of their agents— was revealing what was discussed in that holy of holies, the dressing room, which was traditionally a refuge from accountability.

It had been Darren Lehmann's misfortune to say 'Black [aperture]s!' on the threshold of the dressing room after being dismissed in a one-day game against Sri Lanka.

Had he gone in and closed the door he could have said what he liked, but those fatal few centimetres did him in. He was suspended for five matches for racial abuse.

'What happens on the field stays on the field' is another unspoken code, but it was violated by the unconventional Adam Gilchrist. In a World Cup game against Pakistan in South Africa in 2003, Gilly suddenly rushed over to the square leg umpire and complained that wicket-keeper Rashid Latif had called him a 'white [aperture]'. This was the first recorded case of black-to-white racism, but then Gilchrist was no stranger to 'firsts'. In another game he was pronounced not out by the umpire and he walked. Of course, when he got to the dressing room he was abused by skipper Ricky Ponting for conduct unbecoming to the baggy green cap, but just the same, it was a theatrical coup of startling originality. As David Hookes said of the incident on *Inside Cricket*, 'The last Australians to walk were Hume and Hovell.'

The most ambitious attempt to civilise global cricket was the code of behaviour drawn up by the Australian Cricket Board, with penal powers to be used against anyone yelling out 'Black cunts!' or 'White arsehole!' within earshot of the public. This is the Racial and Religious Vilification Code:

> A player who is participating in a match under the jurisdiction or auspices of the ACB will not engage in any

conduct, act towards or speak to any other player in a manner which offends, insults, humiliates, intimidates, threatens, disparages or vilifies the other player on the basis of that player's race, religion, colour, descent or national or ethnic origin.

That's why there aren't any more Thommos.

When he was asked about being last man out in England's three-run victory at the Boxing Day test at Melbourne in 1982, Jeff Thomson admitted that it still rankled. Trying to hit a boundary to win the match, Thommo snicked the ball into the slips, where it was knocked up by Chris Tavaré and caught by Geoff Miller.

'I wouldn't have minded so much,' Thommo told an interviewer, 'except it was a shit ball and I was caught by two sheilas.'

4

Shouldering arms

I remember my first cricket bat,
Linseed oil rubbed down the blade
With an old singlet,
The crack of the mallet
Along face and edges,
A dream of Benson and Hedges.

from *My First Cricket Bat*, Stephen McInerney

'Cricket is not a body contact sport', runs the old adage, but it has come close to one in recent years, most notably at Eden Park, Auckland, in 1992. Nothing comes as close as a shatterer of illusions. 'All sport is boxing in another form,' claimed Peter Roebuck, but cricket has taken that 'another form' to another level. The oval is a white-collar Colosseum, and violence plays around with many taboos.

Well before then, in 1971, English quick John Snow had caused enormous controversy by colliding with Sunil Gavaskar, who was running between wickets. Did Snowy deliberately obstruct the Indian opener? The press was sure he did and deplored the introduction of physical contact. The crucifixion of Snow followed hard upon his success in Australia in 1970–71, where he bowled England to an Ashes victory, became the first player to be manhandled by a spectator while still on the field, and broke his finger on the old picket fence that was soon to be transformed by advertising signs. After the Gavaskar incident he was never the same player.

Len Hutton was once given out 'obstructing the field', but it is a rare form of dismissal, with Sri Lankan captain Hashan Tillekeratne being the only other player to come close. It is, however, common practice for batsmen running between wickets to place themselves between the thrower and the stumps. This usually means that the fielder will not throw the ball as he is unable to see the target; if he does, the batsman is running in the same direction as the ball, so that if it hits him in the back, it will only be a glancing blow, and he can legitimately turn and sneer at the fielder 'Didn't hurt!' (with Kiwis, it sounds more like 'Dud Nert!'). During a match between England and Zimbabwe, Ian Botham commented approvingly: 'Heath Streak shows all his experience, getting between the fielder and the stumps.' Michael Holding then raised a very pertinent matter when he asked: 'Why is that not obstructing the field?'

In 1981 Dennis Lillee and Javed Miandad nearly came to blows, or rather, to bats and boots. Lillee tried to kick Miandad and the Pakistani, every inch the cheeky Karachi urchin, brandished his bat as if to take revenge. They were separated very quickly and there was no real chance of violence, but the photograph was widely circulated as some sort of evidence of a decline in the behaviour of cricketers. What it depicts is pure play-acting, a travesty of cricket and a travesty of violence. As they might say in LA-land, these guys sure traved it.

The most chilling sight I have seen in cricket happened in the Sheffield Shield final at the SCG in 1985. New South Wales batsman Peter Clifford was going well, accumulating runs and proving hard to shift when 'over' was called by the umpire. Queensland captain Kepler Wessels walked across, ostensibly changing field position, moved in close to the bespectacled Clifford and then whack! He dropped a shoulder into him. This was the most shocking cricket incident recorded by a moving camera, but it went unnoticed—or at least unpunished—by umpires and officials and it called into question their pious remarks about codes of conduct.

In 1989, I described the giant West Indian fast bowlers Curtly Ambrose and Courtney Walsh at the SCG in a test match against Australia as 'walking about as if on stilts' and 'beaming down from a great height at the puny litter produced by the captors of his ancestors' respectively. This was when the West Indies were under the captaincy of Viv Richards and they were in the process of carrying all before them. By 1992, though, they were a divided and fading team and no one, least of all Courtney and Curtly, was beaming.

Former New South Wales spin bowler Gavin Robertson once delivered a Tolstoyan aphorism: 'As a general rule, politics within great teams is minimal, politics in mediocre teams is rife.' When Viv Richards stood down, Malcolm Marshall, as the senior player and no mean tactician, thought that the Windies would take a punt on appointing him its first bowler–captain, but in the event they went for the stylish, elegant and brittle batting wonder, Richie Richardson. It was not a happy bunch who arrived in Auckland for a crucial World Cup game in 1992.

Many cities have shared facilities whereby the football codes play on the cricket ovals in winter, on the geometric principle that a rectangle will fit into an ellipse. Australian Rules remains the only football code in the world not to play on a rectangle, having been designed to be played in a seemingly immovable object—a cricket ground. This was not the case in winter-oriented, rugby-mad New Zealand. Auckland's World Cup cricket venue was Eden Park, a rectangular football ground where an oval had been 'fitted in' with uneven results. One girl in the queue on the footpath wore a T-shirt bearing the legend, 'I'm stumped. Where's the rugby?'

The configuration of Eden Park was an apt metaphor; cricket had to fit in as best it could in a rugby world. The result was a very short boundary at backward point for the left-handed Kiwi opener Mark Greatbatch, who duly sliced and slashed and hit sixes off Curtly Ambrose from what looked like horribly miscued cover drives. The tall paceman was unimpressed and he advanced down the pitch to tell the batsman just what he thought of him. It was one of those grey Auckland days where the sky looks dark and threatening for hours on end, but produces no rain. It played its part in heightening the dramatic events out in the middle, as cricket always looks more edgy under an overcast sky; bright sunlight can bleach all the drama out of a game. Can you imagine that satanic ritual, the State of Origin, being played on a sunny afternoon?

At first the ex-rugby forward Greatbatch stood his ground as Ambrose advanced on him, spewing out non-endearments from a thunderous face. The crowd went quiet and jaws started to drop as it looked as if international cricket's first punch-up was about to take place. Whereas in rugby they would urge potential combatants to have a swing at each other, cricket is very much the science of avoiding violence, of swaying out of harm's way, of behaving like a trapeze artist and living to face another test of courage and coordination. The perceived danger, for all concerned, comes from that little red projectile being hurled at speeds of up to 160 kilometres per hour, not from anyone's fists.

It was obvious that Ambrose was in no mood for reconciliation, so the burly Greatbatch turned his back and walked towards square leg. This had the effect of cranking up the tension even more as the apprehensive and still-silent crowd looked to see what Big Curtly would do. He stopped, muttered a few more oaths in the direction of the retreating batsman, and then walked slowly back along the pitch, past the frozen umpire and towards his mark. The sound from the crowd—a collective sigh followed by rumbling conversations—was quite unlike anything I had ever heard in a cricket ground. They did not want Eden Park to turn into a boxing ring. The match resumed and the Windies, failing to exploit the configuration of this unusual ground, were defeated, effectively ending their World Cup hopes.

Curtly Ambrose stalked off the arena, followed by Malcolm Marshall, who had a more jaunty gait and appeared—it could have been an illusion—to be smirking. The premature death from cancer of this great athlete was a shock to many sports fans, who always provided a buzz in the crowd whenever Eminem was handed the ball. At the press conference after the match, Richie Richardson was grilled about the Greatbatch incident by the *New*

Zealand Herald's Don Cameron, but he would not be drawn on the possibility of players coming to blows on the cricket field, so the rest of us did not ask many questions. I noticed that Richardson's hands were shaking and I thought, 'This poor guy is heading for a nervous breakdown.' In the event, it was West Indian cricket that suffered the breakdown.

In 1995 they lost a home series 2–1 to Australia and that was the end of the nineteen-year 'reign of terror', in which physical intimidation played a big role. They did not bowl Bodyline as such, but they left behind a lot of sore and sorry (and hospitalised) batsmen. The turning point for some came when Curtly Ambrose gave Steve Waugh his trademark glare from close up, and instead of walking away, Tugga inquired: 'What the fuck are you looking at?' Ambrose was incensed and had to be pulled back by his nerve-racked skipper, Richie Richardson. Would Waugh and Ambrose have come to blows if Richardson had not intervened? Waugh said later that it was probable rather than possible and he would not have backed himself. Richardson has never commented, and retired prematurely soon after with chronic fatigue syndrome.

The first inkling I had that the West Indies empire was crumbling came in the breakfast room of a Jakarta guesthouse in that watershed year of 1995. The only cricket I had been playing was the soft-ball indoor variety at the

Australian Embassy with members of the Oz business community. Suddenly there was cricket on the television screen during the *Good Morning Indonesia* (literal translation available on request) show. Curtly Ambrose was bowling, and pounding Steve Waugh, giving him bruise after bruise, and Waugh was just smiling back down the pitch at the giant paceman. The happy-talk hosts of the show stared at each other and gaped at the camera as if to ask: 'This is sport? It looks like a medieval stoning.' They then crossed to Recipe of the Day. *Good Morning Indonesia* did not provide any scores, but there was something about the way Steve Waugh looked at Ambrose that told those of us from the Commonwealth that the world had a new number one cricket nation: Australia.

During their long reign, the Windies had every right to play to their strengths—size, pace, the 22-yard stare—but the flirtation with violence was always threatening to get out of control. In New Zealand in 1980 the issues of match-fixing and codes of conduct collided and the West Indies went home as losers for the only time in the period 1976–95.

Although West Indian cricketers have traditionally had genteel names like Berkeley Gaskin, Seymour Nurse, Eldine Baptiste and Vanburn Holder, from 1976 their tactics were anything but genteel. In the fourth and final test at Sabina Park that year the Indian second innings contained five 'absent hurts' and the Windies only had to

take five wickets to dismiss the whole side. In his book
Sunny Days, Sunil Gavaskar wrote:

> When I faced Holding, I received four bouncers in an
> over and a beamer which Holding pretended had
> slipped from his hand . . . To call a crowd 'a crowd' in
> Jamaica is a misnomer. It should be called a mob. The
> way they shrieked and howled every time Holding
> bowled was positively horrible . . . All this proved
> beyond a shadow of a doubt that these people still
> belong to the jungles and forests instead of a civilised
> country.

Whew! It is just as well the ACB's racism code is not
retrospective or international.

By the time they got to New Zealand in 1980, the
West Indies were widely thought to be invincible. How,
then, did they come to lose the series 1–0? According to
manager Willi Rodriguez, the West Indians were 'set up'
and 'there was no way we could win a test'.

These were the days before neutral officiating and the
Windies bowlers had most of their appeals turned down
by New Zealand umpires who were described as 'patri-
otic'. At one point Michael Holding kicked over the
stumps, and at another, Colin Croft tipped off the bails
as he walked back to his mark. He then bumped the
umpire with his elbow as he ran in to bowl. As they say
out in West Burrumbuttock, 'What a pack of sheilas!' The

culture of cricket and the emphasis on concentration is such that violence is unexpected and seen to be petulant when it does finally surface.

The only Sydney grade player to be suspended in recent years for 'physical contact' was Don Nash, who was involved in an altercation with Richard Chee Quee. Although Cheeks presents as Chinese, there are some hefty Fijians in his ancestry, and it shows, so we can rule out bullying, even though Nashy is a fast bowler. He was suspended for one match only, which suggests either that the physical contact was of a 'ships in the night' nature or the code of conduct enforcement procedures are in the 'flagellation with a feather' category.

'Academic politics are brutal because so little is at stake,' said Henry Kissinger, and the same could be said about some outbreaks of cricket violence. In a World Cup match in Perth in 1992 a jaded and dispirited Australian outfit, who did not make the semi-finals, were easily beaten by Pakistan, who went on to win the Cup. Michael Whitney walked out to bat when the game had already been well lost, and nearly came to blows with Pakistan wicket-keeper Moin Khan, who had sledged 'Whit' about his undistinguished batting record. The clash between the two—verbal, because of interventions—made the head-lines because the match itself was one-sided and uninteresting. There was no 'cauldron' atmosphere with mighty wills colliding; it was a spiteful and catty episode that came to nothing. The weather—it was a hot and humid night—may well have played its part, too. As Gordon Bray once said, 'Temperatures are fraying out there.'

When he was interviewed by Margaret Throsby on ABC Classic FM in 2003, Dennis Lillee was asked the question he knew was coming: 'Has cricket behaviour declined and what can be done about it?' The man once known as 'FOT' (Flippin' Old Tart) gave a somewhat surprising answer. He said that only the introduction of a sin-bin will stop behaviour that goes beyond gamesmanship.

It was Jeff Thomson, the King of Ping, who had been the first bowler to talk about hurting the batsman as a fast bowler's aim. In 1974 he said he aimed at the rib cage and then threw in a 'sandshoe crusher' for variety. With typical Thommo relish, he said he enjoyed making his prey jump about trying to dodge these missiles. Dennis Lillee then said something similar in a book published during the 1974–75 season, and the English press hit the roof. This was tantamount to Bodyline, they alleged, saying that it was surely cricket to aim at the stumps, not the batsman. A cartoon character, an 'Ugly Australian' fast bowler called Terror Tompkins, quickly became a staple in the sports section of one English newspaper.

Charter members of Ian Chappell's Wild Bunch, Lillee and Thomson, were great bowlers who battled injury and finished up with 355 and 200 test wickets respectively. They were also larrikins and pioneer intimidators who forced batsmen to begin wearing helmets and unwittingly ushered in the West Indies era of relentless pounding by a quatrain of express bowlers. If Australia can be blamed for creating a violent approach to the gentleman's game, they were certainly punished for it.

Watching Steve Waugh's new policy towards pain and intimidation in the Caribbean in 1995, as he took bruises on his bruises, was a salutary lesson in adaptation, counter-attack and strength of will. Australia had dished it out during the Chappell era and now they proved they could take it. No one could say that overall justice has not been done.

JOCK ALEXANDER

5

Field chat

'Sticks and stones will break my bones,
but names will never hurt me.'

Children's playground chant from the pre-PC era

'There was always an element of psychological warfare,'
said John Traicos, 'but no sledging, I don't remember any
sledging.'

Traiks was speaking of South African and Rhodesian
cricket in the 1960s. What about the targeting of opposition players? 'Oh, that went on, sure,' he admitted. 'Ali
Bacher was the captain and he told our batsmen that even
if they had made a century, even if they were pushing for
quick runs, they were not to give their wicket away to
Graham McKenzie. But nothing was said to Garth on the
field.'

McKenzie had been South Africa's main danger in previous series, but in 1969–70, under Bacher's regime, he took one wicket, had 333 runs hit off him, and Australia lost the series 4–0. So the targeting had been successful? 'Oh yes, it was very successful,' said the lean and fit-looking off-spinner who represented South Africa and Zimbabwe in test cricket. And what happened to Garth Mackenzie, Australia's leading fast bowler in the post-Davidson era? Were there hard feelings? 'He married a South African girl and stayed there.'

It was Bobby Simpson who first used sledging as a means of defining the difference between first-class cricket and the grade or club game in his autobiography, *Captain's Story*. He played forward and got an edge to his first ball in Sheffield Shield from a Jack Hill top-spinner and set off for runs: '. . . scampering up the wicket, I smiled at Hill as I turned for two. "You lucky little bastard," he sneered, and I knew immediately that playing interstate cricket had none of the happy-go-lucky approach associated with many grade games.'

Brian Booth confirms Jack Hill as an unofficial Shield greeter of the 1950s when he writes of his first-class debut in a Wisden memoir:

In my first Sheffield Shield match against Victoria at the SCG I was batting against the experienced leg-spinner Jack Hill. I played forward, meeting the ball with the full face of the bat. Jack appealed like a thunderclap for leg-before. The umpire rightly said not out. Jack turned towards me and gave a short verbal blast with one or two 'b' words included. I was bemused.

By 2003 sledging had become so much a part of the game that it figured in television commercials. One was for a takeaway KFC lunch tastefully named 'Cricketer's Box'. It featured a nasty wicket-keeper who harps on the fact that the batsman will soon be out and can have something to eat, a variation on Lou Benaud's parting shot to a brash young blade he had just dismissed on a hot day: 'You'll find it's much cooler in the pavilion, son.' The other commercial was for American Express and starred good guy Adam Gilchrist playing a New Zealander who observes to an Australian batsman: 'I've seen better bats in a cave.' ('I've sin bitter bets unner cave,' said the dubbed voice Gilchrist was lumbered with.) These were of course sanitised versions of the more common subjects of sledging: death and sex.

In 1975 New Zealand bowler Ewen Chatfield was hit on the head while batting in Auckland against England and collapsed. His heart stopped and he was only revived by mouth-to-mouth resuscitation. At Christchurch in 1978 English batsman Derek Randall was backing up at the non-striker's end when Chatfield ran in to bowl and suddenly 'Mankadded' him, removing the bails and appealing for a run-out. The umpire had to give it out, as it is only a convention that the bowler should warn the batsman first and only run him out if he persists in backing up too far. Randall had to go, and Chatfield had his moment of unconventional triumph, but he must have known he would join Vinoo Mankad in the Rotten Dirty Scoundrels wing of the Hall of Fame and bring discredit on New Zealand cricket. Chats was not popular with the English team either, and received a memorable sledge from Ian Botham: 'Remember, mate, you've already died once on a cricket field. Anything can happen.'

Sri Lankan skipper Arjuna Ranatunga had a demeanor somewhere between Squizzy Taylor and Adolf Hitler and was known variously as 'Captain Sook' and 'Runner Tunga' because of his propensity for asking for a runner early in an innings. 'Why are you so fat?' he was asked by wicket-keeper Ian Healy (it's always the wicket-keeper). Ranatunga's answer—'Because every time I screw your wife she gives me a biscuit'—has since passed into cricket folklore, even though it involves that staple of all rejoinders, a reference to the sledger's spouse.

Although the Sri Lankan players' wives all looked like film stars, Arjuna Ranatunga did not, and he was monumentally unpopular in Australia, a bona fide black Jardine. He in turn harped on Australia's convict beginnings, sounding almost like an honorary New Zealander. Arjie was fat and petulant, and like most sledgers, had an enormous chip on his shoulder. The imaginary voices inside his head kept saying, 'I'm from a superior class' and then adding, 'Yes, but you're from an inferior race.' The intersection of race and class has bedevilled other sub-continental cricketers when they venture southwards, being black and upper class and playing mainly against opponents who are white and working class. What else can they do but play the convict card?

Australians are generally regarded as the sledgends of the modern game, and the same goes for the women's team, who do not claim any moral superiority. 'Women's tennis is less conflictual than men's,' wrote one goose in an attempt to curry favour with the feminist movement. There is no such word as 'conflictual', and anyone who has gone on the women's tour will tell a more realistic story, especially the competitors themselves.

On their 2001 tour of England and Ireland the Australian women cricketers were subjected to much criticism from opposition teams because of their coarse comments and their fondness for leaving derogatory notes wrapped around sweets for the batters to find. England manager Gill McConway took the high ground when she told the *Guardian*: 'Australia are probably the most un-couth team in world cricket and while we encourage our girls to respond, we do not want any bad language.'

Racist sledging ranges from the mild to the distasteful, from umpire Simon Taufel's muttered aside, 'I bet the

Bangladesh innings won't last as long as their anthem', to the barrage faced by sixteen-year-old Darwin Aborigine Ken Vowles in Adelaide A-grade: 'Are you gunna go back to your camp? Don't you want to get out and find a black slut to make some more black kids? There's a beer waiting for you on the other side.'

This was all light years away from the wordless sledge of Warwick Armstrong during the Oval test in 1921. When a newspaper blew across the field, 'the Big Ship' picked it up and affected to read it. This gave the crowd and the opposition the impression that winning the match was going to be a doddle and he could afford to relax. 'Why did you do that?' he was asked later. 'I wanted to see who we were playing against,' answered the bulky captain. This did not mean he thought the England team was substandard—although it was a bit—it was a protest against the scheduling of the MCC, which tried to wear the Australians out by having them play against county teams as far apart as possible. Armstrong's comment was really, 'I wanted to see who we were playing against *tomorrow*.'

Everyone has heard of the Steve Waugh remark to Herschelle Gibbs, who put down a catch during the South Africa v. Australia semi-final of the 1999 World Cup: 'Congratulations! You just dropped the World Cup,' said Tugga. Equally effective, however, was Clive Lloyd's grassing of a chance from Geoff Boycott in the 1979

World Cup final. Boycott had spooned the ball to mid-off, but the cat-like Lloyd unaccountably failed to hold it. This was a wordless sledge, as it meant the Windies wanted the slow-scoring Boycs to continue and use up so many overs he put England hopelessly behind on run rate. When newspapers wrote that the West Indian skipper had deliberately dropped the ball, the normally litigious Lloydy did not issue any writs. Nor did Boycott, for that matter.

Sledging is supposed to date from the 1964 Percy Sledge hit record 'When a Man Loves a Woman' and the emergence of the vociferous Ian Chappellites ('subtle as a sledghammer') during that time. Although 1946 belonged to the golden era of sportsmanship—as it is now painted—there were a couple of recorded instances of 'on-field comments'. Cec Pepper thought he had trapped Don Bradman leg before in a Shield game and when his appeal was turned down he said in disgust to the Don: 'I don't suppose you're ever out.' Pepper had to play out his career in England after that remark. When Bradman was given not out from a waist-high slips catch during the first test in Brisbane, England captain Walter Hammond was furious. 'A fine bloody start to the series!' he thundered. Poor doomed Hammo also suffered from the Curse of Bradman and did nothing of significance thereafter.

During the Sydney test of that series Sid Barnes was scoring slowly when he heard a muttered comment from a fieldsman that sounded unflattering. 'Stop complaining!' snapped Barnesy. 'You're going to be out here for hours yet.' The eccentric opener was as good as his word and made 234 before he spooned a catch to mid-off and it was accepted. Bradman had earlier been dismissed for 234 and Barnes did not want to overtake him.

Len Hutton was the English Bradman, lauded far and wide as 'a professional *and* a gentleman', but the feted Yorkshireman was not averse to a bit of on-field banter. When Richie Benaud began his innings in front of a holiday crowd at the Scarborough Festival at the end of the 1953 tour he blocked the first few deliveries. 'What's the matter with thee, lad?' asked Hutton, 'Playing for average?' Benaud did not respond verbally, but he then set about the bowling and made 135 in record time, including eleven sixes. The first time he came out to bat in the 1954–55 test series Hutton remarked loudly: 'Here comes festival cricketer.' Benaud made no contribution with the bat during this series.

New Zealander Jeremy Coney was one of many players to protest at the degree of sledging from the Australian team, and devised a method to demonstrate to the crowd and television viewers that there was a whole lot of talking goin' on. He held up a gloved hand and made the rapid-movement duck's beak sign, the yacketyyack, 'there's too much palaver' gesture every time he was sledged. The crowd looked bored and some of them booed. In the 1983 one-day final in Melbourne Coney was dismissed for next to nothing by Dennis Lillee, who saw him off with the same quackety-quack gesture, to cheers from the crowd. It was the last time this kind of hand signal was seen on a cricket field; suddenly it seemed like whingeing in mime. Coney is a renowned public speaker and commentator and no doubt has made good his earnings loss with plenty of colourful Dennis Lillee stories at the 'gents' smokers' which are still popular in New Zealand.

Although crowds would not accept physical violence from the players, and the 'bench-emptying' episodes from baseball have no equivalent in cricket, there is no evidence that the public is anti-sledging. Indeed, crowds do their bit, holding up signs ranging from 'The Fat Lady's Singing' and 'What's the 8.30 Movie?' when one team is struggling to the below-the-belt antics of the fans in South Africa, where a sample sign read 'Ntini's Weenie is Bigger than Bichel's Pickle'.

There is no evidence that the sledge pledge of Manly's grade team in the Sydney competition or the Spirit of Cricket Awards in the first-class game have any great public following. Andrew Ramsay in the *Australian* reassured cricket fans that there would be no 'outbreak of unrestrained gentility' and that the lovable larrikins would carry on much as before. Andrew Symonds told him: 'We're not going to stand there like statues and not say anything to each other. We are fully grown men and at times you will see [*sic*] heated things said.' This neatly scuppered the ideas that sledging belongs in the school playground and that it is some kind of baggage from the Ugly Australians era. As Bertolt Brecht used to say, the bitch is still in heat.

ROCCO FAZZARI

6

No melons for
Mr Gregory

Three's a crowd.

Observer of interstate cricket

Good crowd in.

Bill Lawry at the MCG (rpt)

Syd Gregory once scored a double century at the SCG and a delighted spectator ran out and presented him with a watermelon—an impractical gift, as no doubt the umpire pointed out—but a heartfelt one. On another occasion an habitué of the Hill was 'razzing' Gregory, so the test batsman ran over, jumped the fence and 'jobbed' him. Crowds . . . can't live with 'em, can't shoot 'em.

More than a hundred years later, in an incident that had strong men retching, spectators at the Gabba in Brisbane threw bananas to Sri Lankan spinner Muttiah Muralitharan when he was fielding in the outer. They did not throw them *at* him, they threw them *to* him. No doubt Murali, a solid ex-rugby player, wanted to jump the fence and sort them out, but that barrier is no longer so easy to negotiate, thanks to advertising signs, and there are fines for players who give the finger to spectators, let alone a bunch of fives. No doubt the ground announcer wanted to say 'No bananas for Mr Murali', but that would only incite the yobbos. Murali later said he would not tour Australia again because spectators yelled out 'No ball!' every time he bowled, and indeed three umpires joined the chorus at various points, but many felt the real reason was the bananas, and fair enough, too.

The people only come for international cricket, and interstate games are played in front of empty stands with unhealthy draughts and echoes. One-day internationals attract a full house of streakers, drunks and racists. Crowds . . . what are you gonna do?

They gave the people of Berry, South Australia, a World Cup game on a public holiday and said if they turned up in good numbers there would be more international cricket headed their way, with subsequent flow-ons for the hotel industry and what they like to call the 'local economy'. Was this an incentive or what? In the event, came the day, came the hour, and not all that many turned up. They have not had a first-class game since, and the harrowing yellow plains of the sub-Riverland remain untraversed. Surely the good people of Berry could have put in an appearance, even if they sloped off when the cricket turned uninteresting. Was it not an opportunity for decentralisation? The familiar complaint of small country towns—there's never anything on—would be taken up a week after they stayed away. What was it they said at the Big River Festival of the Arts—Grafton people love to stay away? Would they once again call Berry a 'sleepy township' on the national news? Yes they would! The game was West Indies v. Sri Lanka, and there were no Australians and no 'bad boys' on view. Was that the problem? Or did they just relish the chance to stay away? Crowds . . . who can figure 'em? One of the few spectators at Berry sat there all day reading a thriller. I couldn't see the title, but it was probably *No Orchids for Miss Blandish*. There were no bouquets for Berry in this episode, which was a pity as what crowd there was behaved beautifully and the ground was, as noted, 'picturesque'.

At the Gabba's first England–Australia test, in 1933, the crowd had been somewhat more fruitful and multi-pliable. 'Come on, dears!' a Yabba wannabe shouted during the partnership between Darling and Love. At least the Indian-born Nawab of Pataudi was not playing; in Sydney the real Yabba had called him 'Pat O'Dea' and advised 'Get back to Africa!' Africa? Not even close!

Stephen 'Yabba' Gascoigne was an Annandale realist who sold rabbits from a cart and walked up to the Parramatta Road shops in his red long johns to buy the papers on Sunday mornings. This real-life rabbit-oh is the originator of such standard catcalls as 'Bowl him a piano and see if he can play that' from his stronghold on the SCG Hill. As a barracker he was keener on exposing foibles than on praise and puffery, and had a sharper eye than most. 'Mind your stays, old man,' he shouted at the unusual sight of Douglas Jardine running stiff-backed after a ball. 'Oh, for a strong arm and a walking stick!' he bellowed as Arthur Mailey ran in to bowl in his first test. 'Hurry it up in there with the powder puff, girls!' he boomed across an empty field; the players were late to start in the 1934–35 Australia v. England women's test series. When Yabba died in 1942 a light certainly went out on the Hill. There were other barrackers, of course, and 'Get a hat'—when someone dropped a catch— became a standard, along with 'Have a go, ya mug', but the Hill evolved into a haven for yobbos and for many it was a no-go area, especially when the sky was full of spinning urine-filled cans. It will end in tiers, the doom-sayers said, and they were right. The whole south-east area of the SCG is now covered in tiered seating, under a rather poignant little sign saying 'Yabba's Hill'.

Super-snot Jardine and the glowering Ray Illingworth were the most unpopular English captains ever to tour Australia, followed by Mike Brearley, who—already under suspicion of being an intellectual—was unwise enough to sport an Ayatollah-style beard at the height of the Iran hostage crisis. In rugby, Clive Woodward, dour and prickly coach of the World Cup champions, was the equivalent. Freddie Brown, the bluff and ruddy-faced skipper of the losing 1950–51 tourists, was the most popular English cricketer ever to come to Australia, and had the barrow boys calling out, 'Beautiful lettuce, get your lettuce now, hearts as big as Freddie Brown's.' Is there a pattern here? Yes, there is. Jardine, Illingworth and Brearley won the Ashes on Australian soil, and this was seen as, at best, a breach of hospitality.

Ian Botham was for a time the most popular tourist with Australian crowds, and was regarded as 'an honorary Australian' in ways that Chris 'Tortoise' Tavaré, clean-cut Geoff Miller and the bespectacled Zaheer Abbas could never hope to be. Botham was a 'boofy bloke', a larrikin who liked a drink and a smoke, and was always in and out of hot water on the sheila front. Then came the 1992 World Cup. Botham and skipper Graham Gooch walked out of a cabaret when comedian Gerry Connolly lampooned the Queen, and IB said he was looking forward to raising the Cup high in front of '50 000 screaming convicts at the MCG'. He also consulted his lawyer about suing a columnist on the *Australian*, christened his hotel room 'The Bat Cave' because he refused to leave it at night, allowed himself to be photographed wearing a striped blazer and Panama hat, and went shopping with Elton John. An honorary Australian? He was gradually revealed as being more of a paranoid, litigious, royalist dandy. The crowd booed him at the MCG when England lost the final to Pakistan and he shredded his bat on the wall behind the pavilion. Didn't he know that the mighty ground holds a lot more than 50 000 and convicts were a New South Wales phenomenon?

There was no such change in climate for Richard Hadlee; he was unpopular with Australian crowds right from the start, being the epitome of the melancholic, carrot-arsed Kiwi who would probably seek and accept a knighthood. 'Sir Francis Drake was the last bowler to be knighted,' observed Arthur Mailey (d.1967), but finally the breakthrough came and it was arise, Sir Richard Hadlee. Paddles took 431 test wickets and is indisputably one of the all-time greats, a master of swing and seam, but it is demeanour rather than ability that scores with crowds in the land of Oz. For the lithe, dark, unsmiling, introspective Kiwi who *admitted* to having a nervous breakdown and was a feral abacus to the extent of counting his wickets in batches of fifty, the signs reading 'Hadlee is a wanker' were inevitable.

Lance Cairns, a much less gifted and dedicated crick-eter—but as boofy as a rhinoceros—was an Australian's New Zealander and a popular figure with crowds, especially after hitting six sixes in a one-day final in Melbourne in 1983, which the Kiwis lost after Hadlee had to pull out. The other side of the Hadlee coin can be seen in the reception given to Greg Matthews in New Zealand, where he was booed and jeered every time he went near the ball.

Not just a Westie, but a Newcastle Westie, Matthews developed into a classic Woolloomooloo Yankee, calling people 'man', saying he 'dug' where they were 'comin' from' and referring to the public as 'cats'. Was this 1959 on Radio 2UE with Bob Rogers, Gary O and Lawsie? Yes it was! A brash, flash Aussie with an earring, a toupée and a protruding lower lip, Mo was every New Zealander's nightmare, confirmation that Australians came down from the trees to sell used cars and proof that En Zed had been right to stay out of the proposed Australasian Federation in 1901. Matthews was called 'Mo', short for Moses, because he got lost and emerged from the bullrushes near Cumberland Oval to play his first grade game, but he was no Moses figure to the Kiwis, and unlikely to part the waters of the ditch, as they call the Tasman Sea, and lead them to Australia. (They actually pronounce it 'the Dutch', but not as a tribute to Abel Tasman's national origin.)

There is a pub in Newcastle which had a signed cari-
cature of Wasim Akram, commemorating the day he
dropped in for a visit. It was a very good cartoon and a
quick perusal of the other sports iconography established
that there were no other subcontinentals on view.
Wozzer was an Australian's Pakistani, just as Mohammed
Azharuddin had been a favourite with the outer crowds,
an honorary Australian, a 'boofy bloke', and someone
who'd have a slog and then fumble for words at the interview afterwards. Big, strapping Alpha males, they allayed
suspicions aroused by Zaheer Abbas (and confirmed
recently by Sourav Ganguly) that the subcontinent was
full of devious, smarmy, bespectacled, slim-hipped intellectual snobs. Once the dynamic duo was accepted,
however, doubts started to multiply. Wasim Akram was
photographed wearing glasses, with hair tumbling down
his forehead, looking like a Booker Prize-winning
novelist. Azza left his wife and was seen squiring a
Bollywood actress around Delhi in his Mercedes. Match-
fixing allegations mounted up. Ball-tampering was openly
discussed. Remember those two screaming inswingers
from Wozzer that dismissed Lamb and Lewis and won the
World Cup final for Pakistan in Melbourne in front of
80 000 well-behaved free settlers? The ball had been
tampered with, said Ian Botham, and the circumstantial
case was strong. Mohammed Azaruddhin's newly found
wealth and celebrity was found to have come from

throwing matches, from serving up a stew, from huge payments made by leading figures in the underworld, and he was banned from cricket for life. And he seemed like such a good bloke . . . boofy as all get-out . . . fabulous mumbler at press conferences . . . not in the least bit articulate . . . the first Muslim to captain India after all those effete Hindus . . . a man's man . . . could bring out the big stick . . . the crowds had loved him . . .

Eddo Brandes was a Zimbabwean's Zimbabwean, a farmer who could breeze into town on a Saturday, change out of his muddy boots and into cricket whites, knock up a century in an hour and then take plenty of wickets— all bowled—before breasting the bar for 30 or 40 well-earned beers. In Australia this affable Zimbo was seen as an amateur out of a time-warp, a pie-thrower, a chicken-plucker and a figure of fun. When was the last time someone with a day job played for Australia? Was it 'Wallaby Bob' Cowper? 'Kangaroo Ted' a'Beckett? You'd be going back a bit, back to what Greg Matthews would call 'amateur night in Dixieland'.

Within Australia, there have been more successful cases of adoption. Dean Jones has always been a Queenslander's Victorian, and he never dropped his lairy persona, his Wally Lewis theatricality or the kind of talkative ego-driven demeanour that made him less than a hero to those dour old Vics, who once declared him persona non grata in the dressing room. If Wally Lewis was the Emperor of

Lang Park, Deano was the Regent of the Gabba, a place where they respond to his kind of antics. The author of articles with titles like 'My Best Knock' and an autobiography called *One Day Magic*, Jonesy was confident of his abilities, and not ashamed of pulling focus or admitting to excellence. Maybe the second volume of his memoirs would be titled *I'll Cry Tomorrow*, but this was today. In the course of scoring a century at the Gabba against India he sent for fresh gloves, an aspirin, a glass of water, lip salve, sunscreen and countless other accessories at the end of every other over. The Australian twelfth man was run off his feet by a series of attention-getting devices a two-year-old would not disdain. 'It's me, Deano,' he seemed to be signalling, 'I'm here, I'm batting, I'm on television, not to mention that big screen up there.' Queenslanders, some of whom can be seen wearing a cowboy hat, a Hawaiian shirt, Bombay bloomers and ugh boots, are colourful people who love a bit of theatre, and Deano was given a standing 'ovie' when he reached three figures, mainly by threading the ball through the on-side for twosies, although he did dispatch an early delivery for six. The story is never in the figures, though, for a crowd; Deano was watchable, even if it was never quite clear what he was watchable for. One record Dean Jones did not want to keep was for the slowest-ever interstate century.

In a game between Victoria and South Australia, Shane Deitz looked like taking this record off the man they called 'Legend'. Jones had been commentating on play, but as Deitz approached the milestone he left the press box and took up a position on the boundary, where he became a kind of negative Yabba, cheering every dot ball and urging the batsman 'Don't have a go!' When Deitz duly posted the record-breaking sleeper, he received a standing ovation from Deano, who represented the crowd in almost its entirety—certainly those who were awake.

Although crowd behaviour is demonstrably worse than player behaviour—few cricketers have been shopped for throwing bottles at spectators—it is usually a mistake for players to engage in interaction that is anything other than the lightest of light touches. When Ian Johnson was booed to the echo at the Gabba in 1952 for being a Vic in a test side devoid of Queenslanders, he asked for a sip of Fourex from a spectator, who complied out of curiosity. Did Johnson say: 'XXXX—Queenslanders can't spell beer'? No he didn't! He observed with a grin: 'This Queensland beer's not too bad!' and was instantly cheered. It would be many years before this ground became known as the 'Gabbatoir'.

During the 1985 Sheffield Shield final, Queenslander Harry Frei was sent to field on the SCG boundary and the nearby crowd saw him as their next sacrificial lamb. As he marked out his position with his boot on the ground the spectators got going: 'You're digging your own grave, Harry.' From there it got steadily worse until the

goaded Queenslander finally turned and made a mastur-
batory gesture at the wanquers who had been tormenting
him. This sent them into overdrive: 'You look like an old
hand at that, Harry' was the only printable response.

Remade Queenslanders Allan Border and Greg
Chappell were respected rather than loved by their
adopted statespersons, but Jeff Thomson put a blond streak
through his hair and went completely native. Like fellow
archetypes Paul Hogan and Brian Brown, Thommo comes
from the Sydney suburbs, but no one believes it. In his
current incarnation as a commentator, he comes up with
gems such as 'He's trying to pitch it in the roughage
outside off stump' and attracts 'hi fibes' all round as a
genuine banana-bender. 'That's why those differences
vary,' Thommo once said, and he is right on the money.

Down south, in the Land of the Long White Posts
there are more complex forces at work for the spectator.
At the MCG during Australian Rules games it is the done
thing if you are sitting behind the posts to call out 'How
big's your dick?' a second before the umpire holds his
hands twelve inches apart to signal a goal. On the other
hand, the members' area is the only one in Australia to
insist on ties being worn in the dining room. At the
Gabba you can expect overcooked chokoes and crumbed
cutlets the colour of the Brisbane River, but the MCG
dining room is pinot grigio territory. There is a large and
well-patronised library, generously stocked with classics of

the summer game, but there is also the yobbo haven of
Bay 13, where you can see pretty much what would have
happened if Ned Kelly had lived. Shane Warne is their
once and future king and when they rioted during a one-
day game, the police sent a special emissary to negotiate
with the insurgents: Shane Warne. Can you dye your hair
and drive a Ferrari and still be a man of the people?
Easy . . .

At Adelaide Oval the crowds are much better behaved
and do not carry on as if they 'own' the players. It is here
that the Barmy Army of England supporters really stand
out, with their incessant chants and songs. They had been
very severe on Phil Tufnell, who was a reasonable spin
bowler but in no sense an athlete in the field. When
Tuffers redeemed himself by taking an unlikely outfield
catch, the Barmies went crazy, rushing down to the
boundary to give the man they call 'the Cat' a five-
minute serenade while the rest of the Adelaide crowd
watched in their usual silence.

There are, of course, some eccentrics at Adelaide Oval,
such as the woman who brought an ironing board,
battery-powered iron and a laundry basket full of wash-
ing to the cricket one day and then proceeded to do her
ironing while keeping an eye on play (it was a Sheffield
Shield game). Spectators were divided as to whether
she was making a sardonic comment on the housewife's
lot or whether she was a cricket fanatic just being

enthusiastic. They have never seen anything like Sid Barnes, however.

When New South Wales played South Australia at Adelaide Oval in 1952, Barnes was the twelfth man for the visitors. He emerged at the drinks break wearing a smart suit and sunglasses, with a portable radio and full barbershop grooming service for the players. He combed hair, held up a mirror, sprayed cologne and put on a routine Charlie Chaplin would have envied. Then, when he finished, he walked off to total silence from the crowd. It was an emphatic illustration of the adage 'Life is easy; comedy in Adelaide is hard.'

At the opposite end of the spectrum from sober-sides Adelaide is the Wankhede Stadium in Mumbai. Most people still say 'Bombay' and the film colony remains Bollywood, not Mollywood, but it is advisable to follow the local pronunciation of the stadium. 'One Cardy' is heaps better than 'Wank Heed'. How this stadium remains intact is one of the mysteries of the universe. To signify approval of a mighty deed on the field, members of the crowd light fires, and by the end of the game there can be more than a hundred fires burning brightly all over the mighty Wankhede. When in Mumbai, it is wisely written, go where the sprinklers are.

7

Asterisks and the gladiators

So Lenore* and I got chatting; now she's here to watch
   me batting
But the pitch looks pretty dodgy and the ball's been
   turning square.
Though I know I didn't nick it (as you always do at
   cricket)
Still the fellow at the wicket throws the ball into the air,
With a roar of 'How was that!' he throws the ball into
   the air
And I swear it isn't fair.

from *Edgar Allan Poe at Lord's*, John Whitworth

---

*   no surname or average given

77

Sports people's lives and reputations often hang by a thread, but in the case of Ted Williams, the man himself hangs on a hook in an icehouse while his family disputes the marketing of his DNA. Williams was a baseball great, a rival of Joe DiMaggio's in the 1940s, and his reputation is all his somewhat underachieving relatives have going for them.

The family of Roger Maris has also been active, and their long campaign has been against an asterisk. Maris hit 61 home runs for the New York Yankees in the 1961 season, breaking Babe Ruth's longstanding record of 60. It appears in the books as 61*, however, and the asterisk note points out that Ruth operated in a 154-game season, whereas by the time Maris came around there were 162 games. The Maris family feels it is unfair to highlight this, that their Roger did not have an unfair advantage over the Babe, not every player plays every game, and a record is a record. They want the asterisk dropped.*

In the late 1990s there was an explosion of home-run hitting and the 61* mark has been bettered by Mark McGwire, Sammy Sosa and Barry Bonds. These three are all much more strapping than the lean and hungry-looking Maris, who died of cancer in his early fifties. They have huge biceps and bulging chests and they hit the ball harder and further than anyone had previously, even Babe

---

*   they have had no success so far

Ruth, the 'Battering Bambino'. When an enquiry into steroid abuse was convened in San Francisco, Barry Bonds was asked to testify. Mark McGwire retired under a very dark Flo-Jo* cloud of ill health, while Sammy Sosa's preternatural pectorals have been the target of satire. Roger Maris's family may like to reconsider that asterisk; it has now acquired a new subtext: achieved without the use of performance-enhancing drugs. They should be campaigning for its retention.

Modern medical jokes such as 'What's the best blood pressure drug on the market?' 'Avapro, ya mug!', bear the stamp of that stentorian rabbit-oh, Yabba of the Hill, but Yabba came from a more innocent era where it was a bit naughty that Keith Miller had a whisky and soda instead of a cordial from the twelfth man's tray and Warwick Armstrong would pad up and wait in the bar before going out to bat. In 2002 a Sydney Swans player charged that 75 per cent of AFL players were 'recreational drug users'.

Only two cricketers have been suspended for drug offences in Australia—the Victorian Shane Warne and the Victorian asylum-seeker Graeme Rummans—and there is no evidence that there is anything at all suspicious about the big-hitting and higher number of sixes being seen in

---

* muscle-bound Olympic gold medallist Florence Griffith-Joyner died at 38

the modern game. It may well be that modern batsmen are less inhibited about 'keeping it on the carpet', and in any case, the boundary ropes have been moved in to entice the six-hitters. Both Warne and Rummans had been using masking agents, and nothing clear-cut emerged about drug use by them or any other player, with the possible exception of Stuart Law, who was congratulated on *Inside Cricket* for taking a spectacular running catch and broke up the panel with his grinning reply. 'Lucky I wasn't drug-tested,' said the veteran Queenslander.

Meanwhile, back at the Asterisk Ranch. Its role in cricket is somewhat different from baseball. Whereas in the latter it denotes something unusual or some kind of caveat or catch-22, in cricket it primarily means 'not out'. When Mark Taylor reached 334 against Pakistan in Peshawar he equalled Don Bradman's record for the highest innings by an Australian in test cricket. The next morning Taylor declared the innings closed instead of resuming on 334 and trying to establish a new record. He was congratulated widely on his lack of selfishness and for not wanting to surpass the Don, but he did in fact: his 334* is ahead of Bradman's 334 because he was not out. There is no chance that the Bradman family will campaign for the removal of Taylor's asterisk, so there it stays. The fact that Matthew Hayden posted a new world and Australian record with 380 against Zimbabwe in 2003 is beside the point.

When Sid Barnes got out deliberately for 234 at Sydney in 1946 it was some kind of death pact with his hero Bradman, or an ironic Barnesian comment on the mythic status of the Don, who had been dismissed earlier for 234. Because Barnes was an opener, however, his 234 appears before Bradman's in one of the oddest-looking scorecards in the history of test cricket. 'It wouldn't be right for someone to make more runs than Sir Donald Bradman,' he said, somewhat cryptically, to an interviewer many years later. Described by one writer as a 'turbulent geek', Barnes was famous for his feuds, conducted through his newspaper column 'Like It Or Lump It', and was once told by a rival commentator, 'You could crawl under a snake in a top hat and stilts.' It had been the fashion for Davis Cup teams to have a captain who sported white hair and reclined in creams on a deckchair, so Barnes defined Ian Johnson as Australian cricket's 'non-playing captain' when his wicket-taking capabilities appeared to wane. The asterisk beside Johnson's name in scorecards signifies 'captain', however; there has never been a 'non-playing captain' in cricket, although Mike Brearley came closer than most. Given Barnesy's taste for controversy and surreal sense of humour, it seems unlikely that the 234 was an act of simple homage, although that was how it looked on the scorecard.

A big 'not out' innings is a good way to boost the average, and there is no doubt that Taylor's 334* was a help to him and ended a dry spell in which it was claimed that a 'Tubby Principle' was in operation, whereby he was excused from the need to make runs. Somewhat of a teacher's pet or sacred cow, Taylor had consecutive test innings of 7, 10, 11, 2, 1, 16, 8, 13, 38, 5 and 7 with nary an asterisk to be seen. He was never dropped and eventually retired at a time of his own choosing.

Trying to look behind the cold, hard figures for explanations and human stories of good and bad behaviour is a difficult business, and perhaps the asterisk could be used to help out. Richard Hadlee could carry a few: * cricketer of the year, but refused to share the car prize with his team-mates; ** averaged five wickets a match, but few of the other Kiwi bowlers were likely to intrude ('the Ilford Second XI' said Graham Gooch of the NZ attack at the other end); *** walks like Mary Pierce. Some would no doubt like to see Miandad, Javed*: * never given out lbw in Pakistan; ** played in era before two neutral umpires were mandatory; *** runs between wickets like a Karachi urchin selling dirty postcards. Krish Srikkanth could be more easily seen in action with: * nicknamed 'Three Cans': ** talked incessantly to himself and therefore could not hear sledgers, no matter how loudly they shouted; *** went a long way on one shot—a lofted drug-free straight drive. Jeff Thomson would only need one: * once wrote a book called *Gardening in the Nude*.

When it comes to Australian players, a lot could be explained in the footnotes, such as Bill Lawry*: * 40 per cent of the matches he played in ended in a draw. Adam Gilchrist*: * walked and trekked in South Africa. Steve Waugh*: * 168 tests, exactly ten per cent of the total played at his retirement (1680). Geoff Lawson*: * fast bowler with optometry degree who always said in commentary at the SCG 'the University of New South Wales end' instead of 'the Southern or Randwick end'. In the case of Merv Hughes*, a reverse asterisk could apply. Often portrayed as a figure of fun because of his girth, his gait and his moustache, he has been described as 'the mincing blacksmith' and his bowling approach as looking like 'someone running after a bus in high heels'. The footnote would read: * took 212 test wickets—and this tally would stifle any incipient satire about Big Merv.

For specialist commentators such as Michael Slater and Greg Matthews, asterisks could be used to translate some of their sayings. For example, Slats opined on Fox Sports: 'He never played spin well, Marto*. He had a shocking average in Sydney when it was a real bunsen burner**.' This would then be explained to the viewer as * Damien Martyn and ** rhyming slang for a turner, or pitch that takes spin. Matthews, who speaks like the hipster Kookie in the old 77 *Sunset Strip* television series, needs constant decoding for 'Suicide's Pfeiffer'* (Warne's

---

* 'Suicide' is one of Warne's nicknames and taking 'five fer' is a Pfeiffer.

five-wicket haul) and after the awarding of $US2000 to the Australian team for winning a test match, 'the brothers are making a lot more out of this than two thousand U'.

Perhaps also, with younger readers in mind, the press might like to explain why, having tagged Waugh 'the ice man', they persist with headlines such as 'The Iceman Goeth, Mum Cometh By Train'* for a story about Mrs Waugh travelling to Sydney to see her son's last test.

---

* The reference is to American Eugene O'Neill's 1946 play *The Iceman Cometh*, which has never been professionally performed in Australia. Why is such a remote piece continually referred to? It surpasseth all understanding. In the play the 'Iceman' is Death, which probably would not please Steve Waugh's fans, and the 'cometh' is supposed to have biblical overtones. According to Eric Bentley, the expatriate theatre critic and self-styled 'Bolton Wanderer', it in fact refers to an old American joke, in which a man arrives home from work and calls out to his wife, 'Has the iceman come yet?' He receives the shouted reply: 'No, but he's breathin' awful hard.'

NORMAN MITCHELL

'Reckon we could rustle up a cricket team among the boys to have a go at ian Johnson's mob beffore they get home?'

8

Ward's wards

It was never a gentleman's game.

Traditional (attribution various)

Cricket began as a disreputable game, if historians are to be believed, and has ended up as a disreputable game, if modern prunes are to be believed. In between times, in the Golden Age, there was supposed to be behaviour of the highest order. Well, yes, there was, to a degree, but why did they contemplate bowling underarm to Jack Hobbs in 1924? Some questions just won't go away.

In the late eighteenth century vast areas of England resembled Bay 13 at the Melbourne Cricket Ground. Public drunkenness was common, and there was a pub or 'gin palace' on every other corner. Crime was rife, the courts were packed, and the pressure was only relieved by founding a new society under the sign of the Southern Cross in 1788—called, er, Australia—and sending half the London underworld down there for a visit. Gambling was everywhere to be found in the England of the time, and all kinds of sport were dominated by bookmakers, touts and gangsters. In Dickens's *Great Expectations* there is a fabulous looking racecourse man called Compeyson, whose checked suit and cigar image was common. At Lord's the leading bookies fielded right in front of the pavilion and took bets from cricketers before the very eyes of the public. If anything, Hogarth, who was reputed to be some kind of Captain Sleaze, painted pictures of Gin Lane and environs that were glamorised. And then along came Ward.

William Ward bought Lord's in 1825 for five thousand pounds and set about making cricket respectable. He codified the laws and conventions of umpiring and scoring, got rid of the bookies and persuaded schools and universities to make the game an integral part of the academic year and indeed a cornerstone of the muscular Christian educational philosophy, almost on a par with the sainted game of rugby. The annual fixtures at head-quarters, Oxford v. Cambridge and Eton v. Harrow, date from this time, as does Gentlemen v. Players. Parasols began to appear on the concourse, and Lord's very defi-nitely moved upmarket, if not quite into the Ascot Gavotte class. Lyricists were to follow, however, and cricket was given the romantic, chivalric treatment in the novels of P.G.Wodehouse and Hugh de Selincourt, where the smell of linseed oil and freshly mown grass, the 'pock' of bat on ball, the Devonshire teas, the clusters of well-tailored striped blazers and the saying 'It's just not cricket' were popularised.

Even in Australia, many of us grew up reading school stories about people with names like Mark Latimore, Frank Finnemore, Steven Kingthorpe or Toddy Kay-Knott, who were 'seeing the ball like a turnip' or were dismissed like Psmith's friend Mike, 'who had just reached his fifty when he skied one to Strachan at cover'. Not every book had someone called Strachan fielding at cover, and not every bowler was a villain ('Psmith's slows played havoc with the tail', after all, and Psmith was a hero), but it was pretty standard for the baddie (called Foxy Foulks or worse), or indeed anyone who revelled in beastly behaviour, to be a sacrificial trundler when the hero came out to bat in the book's climactic cricket match. The ball was inevitably 'cut gracefully to the ropes', it 'dashed up against the rails', or 'it landed with a spurt of dust in the road that ran behind the pavilion'. One mighty heroic swipe by Michael Jackson from Wryken (a fictional school, not a California estate) saw the ball end up in a distant paddock, where 'a draught horse nearly had its useful life cut short'. Occasionally, there were ugly duckling stories, where an awkward outsider, who was 'slow to make friends and jealous when they chummed with others' or who 'muffed a sitter' while fielding, found redemption by scoring a century for the school, but mostly the heroes were impossibly gifted and celebrated right from the start. They were always batsmen, the kind of prolific stylist who 'kept out a vicious yorker' from the horrid spoilsport bowler and then 'beat Strachan at cover with a sweetly timed drive that rolled into the pickets with a satisfying "thwack" and brought up the hundred'. Flashman would no doubt have called these heroes 'sporting asses', but they were in the ascendancy and had real-life equivalents in Colin Cowdrey, Peter May and, at a pinch, 'Lord' Ted Dexter. Wardy, what did you start?

William Ward was a politician and a banker, but he was also a cricketer with some big scores to his name— including a relentless 278 at Lord's—and had an outlook that encompassed both the amateur and professional approach. Gentlemen v. Players, or amateurs v. professionals, lasted until 1963, when it ran foul of not only the political thought of the era but of the realisation that all players were now, in effect, professionals. The gentleman cricketer, who had a real job in the City and turned out for the county only every so often, was an anachronism. The last genuninely amateur thought was voiced by Peter May in his 1956 *Book of Cricket*. Musing on a life torn between working for an insurance company with time off for county cricket, and often asked which he preferred,

PM said he broke his umbrella on the way to the office one morning; he was playing a lovely on-drive as he walked along the pavement and 'the ball must have kept low'.

Brian Booth captured some of the flavour of Australian sporting amateurism with his anecdote about Roy Sitch, captain of Bathurst at Country Week, 1950–51. When a batsman fell over attempting a quick single, Sitch could easily have run him out, but he just stood there, holding the ball. When asked why he did not claim the scalp, according to Booth, he explained: 'How could I? He forgot his boots and I've loaned him a pair of mine. They are two sizes too big for him, and he caught his toe and tripped. It would be unfair of me to run him out in those circumstances.' How sporting, and what wonderful rendering of colloquial speech! Ah, they don't write dialogue like that any more.

The Yorkshire professional Wilfrid Rhodes, who was still playing in the 1920s, is famous for his aphorism 'If batsman thinks ball is spinning, then it is spinning'; but his lesser known statement 'It were never a business stroke, the cut' is more revealing of the attitude of a pro in those days, and indeed in these days of containment in the one-day game. County bowling was tight and straight, and there were not many opportunities to play the square cut, so it was not going to help a pro make his living. The 1950s Australian batmen Colin McDonald made most of his runs from cutting, which suggests a more amateurish and free-spirited attitude to bowling in Australia, with more bouncy deliveries wide of the off stump just waiting to be cut, and of course more leggies to torment.

The professional approach to the game has always been around, from the disreputable gambling-and-gin era, through the Golden Age of sportsmanship to the showbiz ethos of today. Two of the most unscrupulous administrators the world has ever seen, Lord Harris and Lord Hawke, manipulated touring schedules to disadvantage the Australian tourists in 1921 and 1926, and laid the groundwork for the ruthless Bodyline philosophy carried out in 1932–33 by Douglas Jardine, who was to some extent 'the servant of two masters'. During the 1924–25 Ashes tour of Australia, Jack Hobbs was the nemesis of the Oz bowlers, and they schemed long into the night about ways to get rid of him. One suggestion, which thankfully was not followed up, was to bowl an underarm delivery. It was not until 1981 that Greg Chappell's miscued gesture of contempt for the MCG pitch saw the century's only underarm delivery. The batsman, Brian McKechnie, and the bowler, Trevor Chappell, involved in this famous and much replayed incident, both became Eric Hollies figures—minor performers in a major incident—although TC had a successful career in coaching and Kechs became a New Zealand selector.

The sporting gestures of good guys Lindsay Hassett and Wally Grout, often lauded as embodying the spirit of cricket, would be regarded as quaint or irresponsible today. As Craig Johnston has said, if a soccer player has the opportunity to commit a professional foul and refuses to do so, he will be dropped. In 1950, when Denis Compton had made 99, twelfth man Sam Loxton was about to bring on drinks when Hassett waved him back, telling him later, 'You never have a drinks break when a batsman is on that score.' In 1964, Australian keeper Wally Grout refused to break the wicket for an easy run-out after a batsman had been involved in an accidental collision with the bowler. This was in a test match against England. Some of his successors, Rod Marsh, Greg Dyer and Ian Healy, have appealed for catches off balls which bounced, and that was considered standard professional behaviour, except by the old-fashioned romantics from the West Indies, who banned poor Heals from their dressing room. Did they buy the imperial dream, or what?

Part of the embrace of team sport by the muscular Christian ethos was its role in the Empire, particularly on the Indian subcontinent, where the locals took to cricket rather than rugby, mainly because of weather and physique considerations, and showed a natural aptitude for the game. This is something that did not happen in Malaya, where the British stayed until 1957 in a country that struggles to maintain a fifth grade/colts standard of cricket and has never looked like producing a test player, let alone a test team. A country with exactly the same population—18 million—and which was vacated by the British in that same year of 1957, when it was called Ceylon, went on to win the World Cup in 1996 as Sri Lanka (or 'Surreal Anchor', as they say on Ten Sports). For the poor old Malays, the pinnacle of sporting achievement remained winning a medal in badminton at the Commonwealth Games.

The subcontinent was certainly different. When the MCC sent a team there in 1951, just four years after independence at a time it was still called 'Injure', Tom Graveney was farewelled by a stay-at-home official who said to him: 'Good luck. Better you than me. I can't stand educated Indians.' As it turned out, Graves went on to have a wonderful tour, playing in many competitive and enjoyable matches, and it was the making of him as a test cricketer.

With Fazal Mahmood leading the attack, Pakistan defeated Australia in a test at Karachi in 1956. This was no disgrace in cricketing terms, as Fazal was one of the world's leading bowlers, but a cartoon by Norman Mitchell in the *Adelaide News* at the time depicted a small island inhabited by thick-lipped natives with a thigh bone lying around (cannibalism lived on in cartoons much longer than in real life) and a white radio operator asking a very long question of his pith-helmeted friend: 'Reckon we could rustle up a cricket team among the boys to have a go at Ian Johnson's mob before they get home?' Clearly there was some work to be done yet on adjusting to the post-imperial age.

Lord Harris was said to be unadverse to running out the non-striker without a warning, yet the practice became known as Mankadding, not Harrissing, after the Indian all-rounder Vinoo Mankad. Things were not much more scrupulous in the Sri Lankan aristocracy. Zoysa, de Soysa and d'Souza are famous dynastic names, but the latest flag-carrier, Nuwan Zoysa, did not do much for their reputation. As the non-striker in the second test at Kandy in 2004, he put his bat down in front of Shane Warne's front foot to try to distract the spinner at the moment of delivery. It was a clear case of chicanery, with the big man's bat being the chicane. Warney was forgiving in victory: 'Zoysa was sent out to try and off-put me, but it fired me up more than anything.' This is, essentially, the 'Didn't hurt!' response from the blond sportsman known variously as 'Suicide' or 'Hollywood'.

Cricket was supposed to be a civilising force in the Empire, but it did not always cut both ways. In a match against Surrey in 1957 the West Indies were sledged unmercifully on both racial and cricketing grounds and were shell-shocked afterwards. They had thought that cricket was a game for English gentlemen, and were not fully aware of the undercurrents of supremacy, gamesmanship and outright cheating. It was one of many stops on the road to Damascus for the Windies, and it culminated in their emergence in 1976 as the most brutally professional of all teams. They made Tony Greig's Englishmen grovel, and as for the rest of the world, well, as Gordon Bray once said, 'They gave their opponents an abject lesson.'

JOCK ALEXANDER

9

The third Hollywood

When Sobers—and Hanif—made a great big score
The cry went up 'Technically a record, sure,
But please sir, take a modicum of solace:
They weren't made against English bowlers!'
Now Lara has broken first Sobers then Hanif
With some scoring that's beyond all belief
But he, too, must face the crunching of molars
'A record, yes, but only off English bowlers!'

from *Lara Boom Day*, Alexander Buzo
(written when Lara made 375, not 400*
but no less true, it is to be hoped)

Hollywood is of course the capital of the film industry, but in recent years politics has begun to imitate many of its rituals. Canberra is known colloquially as 'the Hollywood for ugly people'; egos and press releases are paramount, but good looks, glamour and charisma are not in huge supply. Now that sport has become so much a part of television and top athletes have such a fanatical following, it could become known as the third Hollywood. 'There's no business like show business' ran the old Ethel Merman song, but the venerable Eth has got it wrong. There are businesses that are exactly like show business and professional sport is one of them.

Writing a script for a television series usually involves thinking up names for characters, streets and firms, and it was no different on *Who Do You Think You Are?* When one of the characters had to ring a drycleaners, I named the firm Gregory and McDonald. We were not allowed to use real phone numbers in the dialogue, so when the producers told me what number I could use, I expected them to say, 'By the way, nice try with Gregory and McDonald, Mr Cricket Nut—now come up with something we can use, like Smith and Jones', but they let it stand, and actress Barbara Stephens says 'Gregory and McDonald' in the final cut. No one working on the program had heard of the once-fearsome 1920s pace bowling pair, who now sounded plausible as a firm of suburban drycleaners. It would not have been likely with great combinations such as Larwood and Voce, Lindwall and Miller, Binny and Lal*, Roberts and Holding, and

---

*   denotes possibility of diplomatic inclusion

especially not with Lillee and Thomson, who were so famous they even inspired a cabaret song, 'Miss Lilian Thomson'. The age of the superstar was well under way in the 1970s and it has rolled on ever since.

'My maiden name was Ford and this was often shortened to "Fordie", which is what I was called at school,' author Helen Garner told an interviewer from 'Good Weekend'. Ford is probably shorter than Fordie (6 plays 4?), but the point is nevertheless made, and in the world of international cricket, names that evolve in the schoolyard way, like Warney, Gilly, Haydos, Punter, Pigeon, Bing, Bich, Dizzy, Tugga and Boof have become increasingly recognisable and therefore marketable. The initials intifada of recent years has seen AB, AD, PT, BJ and JC become so widely applied that it is a relief to find Vic Damone was more interested in singing than cricket. Phil Tufnell was known as Tuffers and the Cat, because, as he said, 'I can lick my own——' [manuscript damaged . . . by the author]. Those cricketers with two nicknames, such as Ian Botham, who was Beefy and Guy the Gorilla, will find of course that the negative one is more often applied (except in the case of Tuffers), but they are still in front of the players who have not yet become stars. A headline in the *Australian* in 2004 read 'Symonds, Gilly charged with dissent', because nice-guy Adam Gilchrist is a superstar known far and wide by his nickname ('Geelly' in Colombo) and English-born Andrew Symonds has struggled to establish himself. Perhaps one day Symonds will draw level and it will read 'Symo, Gilly charged with dissent', but the only way the third possibility could emerge would be in this context: 'Gilchrist, Symo charged with murder'.

Two of the biggest stars of West Indian cricket are Michael Holding and Brian Lara, and they conform to the casting stereotype of immensely tall, fleet-footed fast bowler and short batsman with narrow, watchful eyes. Holding is now the leading commentator for matches involving the Windies and Lara has been their captain on and off since the mid-1990s. Their only problem is that they hate each other. 'He's soft and selfish,' sneered Holding, while Lara's thoughts on Whispering Death involve wishing he would live up to his nickname. Their television interviews are masterpieces of froideur, each silently thanking the height difference for an excuse not to lock eyes, with Lara directing his answers at the buttons on Holding's shirt. They also highlight the problem of the star system: clashing egos. Let us not forget what Roger Waugh said when the Australian of the Year and all-round good guy Mark Taylor retired and handed over the captaincy to number one son Steve: 'He should have gone a couple of years ago.'

Hanif Mohammed's 499 was for many years the most runs made by a batsman in a first-class innings. Hanif was run out going for the 500th and was heartbroken, but was consoled by team-mates with 'no one else will ever get close'. Brian Lara eventually broke the record with his marathon innings of 501, but there was no cheering from the older West Indies brigade. They think Lara—who also held the test record for years with 375 and then again with 400 not out—has buried the spirit of Caribbean cricket with his superstar excesses. He has a Hollywood-style mansion and a string of cars and model girlfriends, but the once-feared Windies are now losing series 5–0, despite the presence of Clive Lloyd as manager, coach and secular priest.

Before Bobby Simpson became coach of the Australian team they did not have one. Simmo was replaced by Geoff 'Swampy' Marsh and then Queenslander John Buchanan was given the job. Peter Roebuck said he was in no doubt that Buck was by far the best of the three, but PR did not appear to take into account that the job was now quite different; the coach has been stripped of selecting powers but still has to sort out all the ego problems. 'Man-management' used to be the job of the captain, and was held to be a large part of Mike Brearley's success. On tour, the captain, vice-captain and 3IC, and then later, the coach, used to form a selection committee in situ, but in 2001 this was changed in a grab for power by ex-players, and the selectors themselves went on tour, moonlighting as commentators. At one stage during the 2002 Australian tour of South Africa, the commentary box was staffed entirely by selectors: Allan Border, Trevor Hohns, Mike Procter and Omar Henry. No doubt they all thought Buck was doing a great job 'below stairs' and laughed about that sissy ethical stuff called 'conflict of interest'. In Sri Lanka in 2004, selector Allan Border was commentating during a tense period of the first test when Matthew Hayden suddenly played a reverse sweep. Border was livid. 'If I had a cattle prod . . . well, I can't tell you what I'd be doing with it,' said AB as the indiscretion was replayed. The time may be coming when a player can be dropped from a team on air, live, by a commentator. The selectors, who are all ex-players, are now the most powerful force in cricket and there is no telling when their empire may acquire boundaries.

The word 'star' has become as corrupted as 'legend', and usually means neither. Marlene Dietrich was relent-lessly puffed by sections of the press, but in her 30-year career every one of the films in which she played the lead was a flop. She was a star, she was a legend, insisted the critics and other hot-air merchants, but when a film in which she had a smallish part—*Witness for the Prosecution*—finally became a hit in 1958, it was obviously the leading actors, the script and Billy Wilder's direction that were responsible. Similarly, Woody Allen is given the star treatment, but he is an appalling actor (the 'Woody' is obviously short for wooden) and his films flop badly, year after year. If he is a star, why does no one go to see him? Conversely, Dean Jones was a match-winner in one-day cricket and lived up to his nickname 'legend', but he had to anoint himself a star with the title of his book, *One Day Magic*.

Brian Lara and Sachin Tendulkar are seen as the great stars of the modern era in cricket, but when Lara blasted a record 28 off one over by Robin Peterson in South Africa, he was in no danger of hitting a spectator. What we heard was the echoing sound of ball hitting bat followed by the echoing sound of ball hitting fence or empty seat. Lara is a multi-millionaire from sponsorships and contracts, but this first test match in 2003 proved he is unable to draw a crowd in South Africa. Leading a divided and substandard West Indian team to defeat after defeat ensured that the attendance did not improve, despite the superstar's presence, while commentary from ex-players Ian Bishop and Daryll Cullinan meant that as an entertainment package for television, this was a frost all round. It was devoid of competitiveness as sport and the coverage had no journalistic value whatsoever. Tendulkar has been feted in his homeland and described in the *Age* as 'the best batsman since World War II', but his long series of low scores in Australia has not made him a drawcard, despite the spectator signs reading 'Sachin music'. In the Boxing Day test in Melbourne in 2003 there was more interest in the rival skippers, Waugh and

Ganguly, and consternation when they both had to retire hurt, courtesy of the MCG pitch.

It is of course drawing a long bow to suggest any comparison between cricket selectors and film producers, but many in showbiz had to dip their lid to the Waugh swansong season of 2003–04. This was showmanship of the highest order and it was, as *Variety* would say, a 'box office bonanza'. The selectors, breaking yet again with precedent, announced Waugh as skipper for the four tests against India, followed by his retirement. Brilliant! The crowds for Tugga's farewell tour of duty were at capacity everywhere, and when he got injured in Melbourne the SCG caterers must have had their hearts in their mouths. At the press conferences where the unprecedented announcements were made, the traditionalist Waugh mumbled manfully that if he played badly he would of course be dropped. No one laughed, and many an old stager murmured, 'Full marks, Tugga. Full marks.' No one in Australian cricket history has been appointed captain or indeed player for so many tests in advance, but what the hell, it certainly played with the punters. In 2003–04, an ageing Steve Waugh meted out a lesson to faltering superstars Lara and Tendulkar: you have to have a good script . . . oh, and a winning team.

10

Liberal boofheads

That's not a nice feeling, when it goes between your legs.

Tony Greig, Channel Nine

Commentators have long been the butt of sports comedy, and some live in terror of making a terminal mistake. The media was the target for so many years, but it did not teach them any sympathy for victims. The most vociferous condemnation of player behaviour in recent years has come from the media.

Bill O'Reilly was one of the greatest spin bowlers of all time, and it is a minor irony that the American cable TV personality of the same name calls his program, *The O'Reilly Factor*, a 'no-spin zone'. The American O'Reilly has a much more colourful turn of phrase than his Australian namesake, and he once memorably commented on changed security arrangements for the Statue of Liberty: 'You can visit Liberty Park, but you can't go up the Lady.'

The Factor's main brief is to keep out the spin doctors and publicity directors and correct the mainstream media's liberal bias by providing 'fair and balanced' coverage. What Big Bill would make of the sports pages of Australia's newspapers is probably unprintable. Liberal bias and editorialising are rampant, and as Louis Nowra said when researching his Shane Warne biography: 'Reading through newspaper pieces on him is to trawl through some of the most pompous, sanctimonious articles and tall poppy bashing I have ever read.' Was it always like this? We shall see.

The Roy Murphy Show was a comedy about a sports commentator with a speech impediment (don't ask how he pronounced trots; he would have said 'harness wacing' if the term had been in use then) and it premiered at the Nimrod Theatre in 1971. Ron Casey, often called 'Wan', came to see it and later rang me to say how much he enjoyed my dramatic handiwork. A few years after that I wrote a series of articles for the Fairfax press on tautology that ran from 1977 to 1983, and the chief target here, Rex Mossop ('He seems to have suffered a groin injury at the top of his leg', 'They're not making much forward progress'), was another commentator who took the humour in good spirit.

Sometimes the bloopers came out of a perfectly logical sequence of thought, as when Tony Greig was watching a replay of a spinning ball coming off the bat and bouncing between the batsman's legs towards the stumps, which it just missed. 'That's not a nice feeling, when it goes between your legs' may sound in isolation like a line from a *Carry On* film or a parody of a feminist poet such as Taslima, but it was an apt comment on the probable state of mind of the batsman on screen.

As more and more sports comedy appeared, there was still satire on the commentators—the *Twelfth Man* being an obvious example—and even in top-rating shows like *Fast Forward*, there was a sports commentator, Pixie-Anne Wheatley, who lived on far longer than her inspiration from American television, entertainment compere Dixie-Ann Whateley. Slowly and subtly, however, sports comedy moved into the field of satirising the players, and quickly and loudly some ex-players decided to convert their party pieces into professional showbiz. Greg Ritchie cranked out the vindaloo wind jokes as Mahatma Cote, while Matthew Johns metamorphosed into the moustachioed king of the geeks, Reg Reagan. In this overheated atmosphere of sport as de facto entertainment, something had to give, and it was good humour.

Commentary in the 1950s was very much organised around the what and the why. The ball-by-ball man, Bob Richardson or Alan McGilvray, would tell you what

happened, and at the end of the over, the expert commentator, usually South Australian Alban 'Johnnie' Moyes,
would tell you why. Not all the ball-by-ballers were
straight up-and-down the wicket types. John Arlott would
concentrate on painting verbal pictures, while Charles
Fortune would vary his pitch, talking as if to his wife in
the morning session, when more women tuned in, and
then gradually becoming more matey in the afternoon as
the male listenership increased. Player behaviour or codes
of conduct were unknown topics, and it was all about the
cricket, with off-field indiscretions—sexual, financial,
gastronomic—of both players and commentators not
being on the agenda. If there was a motto to sum up this
philosophy, then 'not a word to Bessie' was the operative
formula.

In his 2002 Tom Brock Lecture for the University of
New South Wales, Alan Clarkson spoke of his mentor
Tom Goodman at the sports section of the *Sydney Morning
Herald*. It had been Goodo's policy never to say anything
disparaging about a sportsman and Clarko said he had
tried to do the same during his long career at the paper.
It would have been inconceivable for Goodman to have
labelled Ray Lindwall 'the biggest prat of 1953' or for
Clarkson to have written about the nude odyssey by a
rugby league player through the streets of Ilkley, Yorkshire.
'The Man in the Bowler Hat' was claimed to have been
Johnny Raper and later revealed to have been Dennis

Manteit, but not by Clarkson. The *Sun-Herald* description of Glenn McGrath's outburst in Antigua, 'Doing a passable impression of a raving lunatic, McGrath's face went baboon's-bum red as he screamed . . . ' well, you know the rest. Tom Goodman would have been sick if he had ever read of an Australian sportsman being treated with such disrespect. This is what Clarkson said about Goodman in the Brock Lecture:

> Tom worked on the principle of boosting—and not knocking—and I am certain you could count on the fingers of one hand the number of times he criticised a player's performance. The toughest criticism he made was something along the lines of 'Joe Blow did not play as well as he usually does'. In essence, Tom told his readers what actually went on in the match and his advice to me was basic: 'Don't try and con the public, they know as much about the game as we do.'

One of many 'What would Tom Goodman think?' exercises pits him together with one of today's hot shots, who calls the public disrespectfully 'the punters', to discuss the group sex phenomenon in rugby league and Australian Rules. Goodman believed sport was character-building and that sportsmen were ambassadors, people to be admired. Cricket teams definitely did not consist of 'Eleven Toey Humans', and groupies were hardly a part of the Goodman Doctrine. It is to be hoped, for poor old Tom's sake, that the *Sun-Herald* is not the paper they read in heaven.

There was no mentorship or hero worship involved in the ABC/BBC 'foreign exchange' program, whereby Alan McGilvray was the Australian commentator in Britain and John Arlott (and then others) were the ABC's English component for Ashes tours. Arlott and McGilvray did not like each other and indeed Arlott did not like Australia, declaring after the 1954–55 tour that he was never going back. The big chill began when he asked for a bottle of Grange Hermitage and the waiter at the hotel in Adelaide brought one out with the immortal words: 'There we are, sir. Been in the fridge all day for you.' Apart from the usual vicissitudes of a gourmet and wine connoisseur travelling in the Aeroplane Jelly ethos of 1950s Australia, Arlott was disconcerted by the egalitarian behaviour of his hosts, the rumoured internal spelling of his name as 'Arlott, and the standard of service at country hotels. When brought an early morning cup of tea by a maid he was supposed to have been asked: 'Did you want three sugars?' 'Oh, no,' he shuddered, and then got the firm reply: 'Well youse had better not stir it, then.'

The style of broadcasting in that era and the (reported) events that befell the broadcasters were quite different fifty years later. On ABC Radio in the noughties the what man still did ball-by-ball, but the why guy butted in whenever he liked. The difference in off-field life was perhaps best summed up by a moment on ABC Radio in 2002. Peter Roebuck had just been in court giving evidence in a bondage-and-discipline case, when he was joined at the microphone by Jim Maxwell, who observed: 'The crowd are enjoying this spanking batting.' It was a Freudian slip that many keen judges rate the best of all time.

The advent of Channel Nine into televising cricket in 1977 saw the end of the what and the why, at least on the box. All the commentators were ex-players and were largely bound by the Mates Act, under which the indiscretions of current cricketers were not reported and certainly not moralised upon. Even in the West Indies, where the best commentator by far was a non-player journalist, Tony Cozier, the ex-player mafia gradually took over, and colourful personalities like 'Reds' Perreira ('Welcome to Pert for the tird test . . . ') disappeared, to be replaced by former fast bowlers who made the cricket about as interesting as it was when they were walking back to their marks. This gave an opening to the print media to concentrate on what was left to them, and the sports gossip column was born. They claimed their first victim when Mike Gatting was forced to relinquish the England captaincy because of evidence-free press reports that he had 'importuned' a barmaid at the team hotel and 'occupied the crease'.

Sports comedy was meanwhile proliferating, with shows like *This Sporting Life*, *The Back Page*, *The Dream* and *The Fat*, which attracted high ratings, at least initially. Fatally, however, they crossed over from satirising commentators to criticising player behaviour. Stars like Greg Norman became 'the Great White Fish Finger', and much scorn was heaped on 'Little Lleyton' Hewitt and Shane 'Hollywood' Warne. Neutral personalities who never expressed anything, like Ian Thorpe and Cathy Freeman, became teacher's pets, with nary a word of criticism or satire, whereas forthright characters like Arthur Tunstall and (until the day before he died) David Hookes were endlessly mocked for being reactionary. If a pet left an older spouse with cancer and ran off with a younger film star, there would be nothing but praise. If an Italian designer of predictable sexuality coughed up for an embarrassingly stage-managed world tour of personal modelling appearances by a pet, that was just great. Did the public go along with all this? A publisher paid an advance of more than $500 000 for the Freeman memoirs, which became a book that attracted rave reviews and stiffed in its first week. It hardly sold a copy even when it was heavily discounted and then remaindered. The huge crowds that Norman draws (and not just when Hewitt caddies) suggest that public opinion is light years away from the critics and the editorialisers. The more the sports pages denounce athletes as villains, the more the public regards them as heroes, and the wider the gulf between the sportswriters and the consumers becomes.

The sporting public did not think Glenn McGrath was 'the biggest prat of 2003'. They think he is one of the greatest bowlers of all time and regard him as a hero.

Peter Roebuck deplored the knocking trend and excoriated the debunkers in the Fairfax press: 'Nothing irritates sportsmen more than the sound of snobs portraying them as simpletons.' This was brave stuff, but Mike Carlton embodied the more common media view of things in his column about the Armani-clad Ian Thorpe: 'When athletes of his stellar status are thinking of little else but their next Ferrari and the trophy girlfriend, Thorpe is quietly developing a social conscience.' There was a scene in the old television series *Dr Finlay's Casebook*, in which the good doctor points to his degree framed on the wall and asks himself: 'When will I realise that having this does not give me a licence to preach?' That scene would be unthinkable in today's Age of Opinion and any scriptwriter who wrote it would be sacked.

Liberal boofheads had another fine moment when Denise Annetts complained that the Australian women's cricket team had too many finger-spinners. After scoring a century (157 not out), she was dropped in 1994 because, she said, of her heterosexuality. Surely this would make her a heroine, a whistleblower, someone who was being bullied and discriminated against, an all-round good girl with priceless victim credentials—but no, not on your nelly. The liberal bias in the sports pages was such that she emerged as the villain of the piece and there was no campaign for an open enquiry into her charges that the selection of teams was controlled by some kind of lezbollah. Women's cricket, which had been getting more and more games on television and was making big strides in popular interest, has never recovered from the Annetts controversy. The public simply does not think the best team is on the field, and test matches are now reduced to one paragraph in some newspapers for a day's play. As for televised matches, that bird has flown.

Meanwhile, on televised men's cricket, ex-players reigned, and theoretically viewers had the why and the why all the time. Unhappily, however, this did not lead to any increase in wisdom. Why did Matthew Hayden suddenly blossom as a test player after ten years on the fringe, condemned as 'only a state player'? Was it improved footwork? A growth in confidence? A decline in world bowling standards to the level of state games? The fact that he gets first crack at these pie-throwers? All the why guys gave us was the what. They said he had improved. Yep, he had got better, they emphasised. What about his opening partner Justin Langer, who was also having a picnic against slow and friendly attacks? Tony Greig speculated: 'It's almost as if he's made a concerted effort to improve his overall run rate.'

Sports scandals happen at regular intervals, and the story is never broken by ex-players, who are bound by the code of omerta, or silence. The Warne–Waugh betting cover-up was exposed in a brilliant piece of journalism carried out by the *Australian's* Malcolm Conn, but a leak from the presses enabled David Hookes to be the first to mention it on his radio program the night before the story was published. Technically, then, the story was broken by an ex-player, but only in the sense of stealing material and airing it first. It was such a hot piece of work that it was almost inevitable that there would be a controversy attached to its premiere.

Once a scandal—usually, but not always, involving Warne—is aired, there is a widespread feeling of horror and anger, especially as our children and grandchildren look up to sports stars and imitate them. Then the liberal boofheads get going with their moralising puke, and many people end up sympathising with the guilty star. After one of Warney's phone-sex scandals, a broadsheet scribe said: 'They should take his mobile phone away from him.' This is actually a democracy we are living in, with laws relating to private property, but you would not think so after hearing some of the scandal coverage. Athletes used to be treated like children and subjected to undemocratic measures in the previous amateur era when officialdom reigned over them; there were gags, fines, curfews, sponsorship bans, chaperone provisions, and in loco parentis stuff that went way over the top. Dinny Pails was even forced to eat a quota of lamb chops per day by Davis Cup selectors in 1946. If mobile phones had existed, then officials would have had the power to confiscate them. Now players have the whip hand, just like Hollywood stars of the post-studio era, and they often behave badly. It is, in fact, their democratic right.

It is not an uplifting experience to see mindless conservatism replaced by mindless liberalism in just one generation, but it is happening nonetheless. A few years ago you could hear Neanderthal coaches in gabardine overcoats saying of Islanders, 'The darkies'll turn it up as soon as there's any pressure' and troglodytes like Noel Coward proclaiming, 'Women should be beaten regularly, like gongs.' Now we see Aaron Baddeley and Matthew Hayden criticised and ridiculed for expressing their Christian beliefs. Badds and Haydos appear to be doing no harm to the population at large; shouldn't they be given the same rights as Thai tennis player Paradorn Srichaphan? No sir. Srichie is a Buddhist and he should be granted freedom of religion.

When the broadsheet newspapers imitated the tabloids and concentrated mainly on extra-curricular material, their sporting judgements grew a little more suspect, which is often the case with moralisers and sensationalism. Being an expert is never easy, and sport can be unpredictable, but it was an especially cruel spectacle when one paper judged Indian bowler Agit Agarkar (unaccountably pronounced 'a ghurka' on Channel Nine) to be below international standard on the eve of the 2003 Adelaide test. Swinging and seaming it all over the place, AA took 6 for 41 in a match-winning performance. Was it a fluke? A couple of weeks later in a World Series Cup match against Australia he took 6 for 42. They were certainly starting to get to him.

JOCK ALEXANDER

11

Box office saboteurs

What use is this ritual, held
On a circular meadow
With men arranged in clusters, some
Almost out of earshot?

from *A First View of Cricket*, Jamie Grant

The evolution of cricket into a branch of show business, replete with big money, big egos and sex scandals, has not been applauded by all. The purists have been offended, it has been said. I have never met an offended purist, but then I have been to Adelaide many times and have yet to meet an upset burgher. 'This will upset the good burghers of Adelaide' is the catchcry of arts journalists when an avant-garde play is scheduled for the City of Churches, but, comes the day and comes the hour, and there is never a burgher to be found, upset or otherwise. Similarly, whenever an innovation in cricket is announced, from coloured clothing to a video umpire, we are told: 'This will offend the purists.' Did these purists ever watch Trevor Bailey bat or Mike Hendrick bowl? Did they count the seagulls as the West Indian fast bowlers walked back to their mark? Have they ever seen negative batting, slow over rates, useless rest days, time-wasting tactics and rain-ruined tests? If they have, they will welcome each development that takes cricket down the showbiz path. Showing a complete disregard for the paying customers is bad behaviour of the same order as on-field tantrums, sledging, chucking, watering the wicket and almost, but not quite, fixing matches.

'Ladies and gentlemen, the test score is 2 for 105,' announced Bishop Moyes, brother to Johnnie, at the conclusion of speech day at my school in December 1958. There was laughter from the parents and a cheer from the students, as many of us knew Australia was batting and only needed 147 overall to win. This last day of the first test in Brisbane was the only one to bring cheers. A couple of days before, when Trevor 'Barnacle' Bailey scored 68 in seven and a half hours, many spectators who had come down from the country left the Gabba vowing never to watch test cricket again. Australia reached the target with only the two wickets down, and it was Norm O'Neill who did the damage with a 71 not out that was full of his trademark drives and cuts to the boundary. At the other end, Jim Burke, who had opened, kept the Bailey spirit alive with a single-dependent 28 in 250 minutes.

Bailey and Burke were box office saboteurs of the highest order, but it was their South African contemporaries who were the true masters of the art. Just to look at their names or hear them out loud is almost enough to suggest sloth and ennui—Endean, Waite, McGlew, Bland. Russell Endean was known to his team-mates as a tough fighter, a sheet anchor, a real Mr Reliable and an engaging tour companion. To the rest of the world he was 'Endless' Endean, a defence-oriented batsman newsworthy only for the peculiar dismissals he got himself involved in.

Standing in as wicket-keeper for John Waite in the final test against England in 1951, Endean was about to catch a big slow floating snick from Len Hutton, when the Yorkshireman suddenly had another swipe at the ball. He missed, but succeeded in baulking the keeper, and when the ball hit the ground the South Africans appealed. Hutton was given out 'obstructing the field', the only time this has happened in test cricket. In a test against England at home in 1956–57, Endean was batting and played the ball into the ground. It bounced up and back and headed for the stumps, whereupon he cuffed it away with his glove. He was the first test batman to be given out 'handled the ball'. To date, there have been four others, but Endless has a secure place in history.

Cricket was often reduced to a stalemate in the 1950s and 1960s, with bowlers dropping it short of a length and batsmen not attempting to score. Footwork became a distant memory. At one stage in the 1957–58 series when Jackie McGlew—whom John Traicos names as a respected and influential figure in South African cricket—actually scored a run, Australian wicket-keeper Wally Grout asked why the crowd was applauding without any sense of irony. 'He's just broken a record,' he was informed. 'Must be a long-playing record,' muttered Grout. For Australia, Bill Lawry, after a bright, match-winning start to his test career, settled into his longtime role as 'a corpse with pads on', as Freddie Trueman called him. On the last day of the fifth test in Sydney in 1963, Phanto scored 45 not out in four and a half hours and buried the series in an unmarked grave. 'I could have throttled Lawry,' said Betty Archdale, headmistress of Abbotsleigh, who brought a school party to the ground. Lawry, the dour batsman who was a good Victorian and a racing pigeon enthusiast, was later to remark with undoubted truth: 'I have made more friends overseas from pigeons than from cricket.'

The first day of that test was made a living hell by Ken Barrington, who compiled 101 for England in just under six hours, despite jeers, slow hand-clapping and entreaties to 'have a go' from a disenchanted Hill. On a good batting wicket against a moderate attack, Barro treated half-volleys with great caution and was only intent on carrying out that faintly salacious cliché, 'occupying the crease'. Richie Benaud's wonderful aphorism—'The batsman with the best footwork is the batsman who doesn't believe the wicket-keeper exists'—refers to those unafraid to make Trumper-like leaps down the pitch to drive, oblivious of any stumping chance. Benaud's wise words did not come into play here, as Barrington's idea of footwork was to anchor his back toe inside the crease and push out with bat and front pad together to smother each delivery. There was no stroke play, no shot-making, and no enter-tainment for the large and expectant crowd. This is bad behaviour on a scale equal to the most eye-popping Ian Botham or Shane Warne escapade, and something had to be done about it. Later in 1963, the Gentleman v. Players annual game was abolished, bringing one era to an end, and the first one-day competition, the Gillette Cup, for English county teams, began. 'Sacrilege!' thundered some, but those who had suffered through the tedium of the 1962–63 Ashes series were ready for innovation. The following year, Barrington was dropped from the English test team for scoring too slowly. The policy of the great snails of the 1960s—Lawry, Boycott, Hanif Mohammed— was more akin to the American military term 'area denial', and gradually laws were changed to make sure the spirit of cricket could be enforced by the umpires.

After Brian Close's classic time-wasting epic of 1967, when he saved a match for Yorkshire, a new law was brought in, whereby fifteen overs had to be bowled in the last hour of a match. Before Close's effort, it had been assumed that it was not in the spirit of the game to slow it down to the point where what had seemed an obvious victory could be denied by a captain changing the field placing after each delivery. With the new law, games scheduled to finish at 6.00 p.m. inevitably went to 6.15, such was the slowness of the over rate.

When it became obvious that teams could slow play down well before the last hour, yet another new law was brought into being: teams had to bowl fifteen overs an hour for the entire match, which meant 90 overs a day. How the West Indies squawked! This was aimed at bringing their reign to an end, they claimed, as under the new law with their quatrain of express bowlers operating off their long run-ups, they would be lucky to get home before the streetlights came on. The 90-over quota did come in, however, and pretty soon the day's play stretched until 6.45 p.m., playing havoc with television schedules. Steve Waugh faced the last delivery of the 2003 Sydney test at 6.39 p.m., after English captain Nasser Hussain spent two minutes changing the field, packing the off-side with seven men as the shadows grew. The fact that

Waugh hit this last delivery through the covers for four to bring up his century made it all the more memorable. Hussain had played his villain role to perfection, and it was the first time anyone could remember that time-wasting had increased the drama of the occasion.

Commentating with Alan Donald on a South Africa v. England test match in 2003, Ian Botham looked at the clock and remarked: 'Ten to seven, and they're still playing cricket! Most sensible people are in the bar at this hour, which is where you and I should be, AD.' If introducing 90 overs a day was meant to lift the rate at which they are bowled, then the law has not quite worked. Who is to blame? Vijay Manjrekar was commentating on a game under overcast skies in the 2003 World Cup, when Zimbabwe was rushing to bowl the minimum 25 overs to make a game of it with easybeats Namibia: 'Seven overs in fifteen minutes. So you see, over rates are in the hands of the cricketers.'

The one-day game has been introduced to provide a bit of showbiz for the summer sports consumer, and it has been largely successful. Even here, though, the time-wasters are hard at work, returning the white ball on the bounce so it gets discoloured on the square, and then waiting, waiting, waiting around while the umpires change it to a whiter-looking equivalent. Yuvraj Singh success-fully wasted almost five minutes when he hurled himself across the square to field a ball and landed on his hip during India v. Australia in 2004. Rain was threatening, and only 21 overs had been bowled; the Indians were behind and wanted to abort before the 25-over mark, which made it a game. The performance of Yuvraj Singh, writhing around clutching his hip and being stretchered off with elbow pointing heavenwards, may have been pure Bollywood, but it did not save India. Only a few drops of rain fell and Australia passed the 25 overs. After the game the supposedly stricken Sikh could be seen gambolling about like a spring lamb. He could hardly have been reprimanded by his captain Sourav Ganguly, who has taken time-wasting into the realm of pure psychology. Goolies is always late for the toss, believing it will unsettle the rival captain. During the Singh histrionics on the field, Ricky Ponting, who was batting, complained to the umpire about time-wasting and got involved in a prolonged discussion. When the game finally resumed he was out first ball; Ganguly could have claimed: 'We were not wasting time, we were trying to break Ponting's concentration.' Those who hung around after the game to yell out 'How's the hip, Yuvraj?' may have been striking a blow for consumers' rights, but they could be sure a blow was coming in return; there are ways yet undiscovered of wasting time on the cricket field. 'Love the short stuff but can't wait for the traditional game?' asked an ad on Foxsports, which is clearly the servant of two masters. There may be few in the crossover audience for one-day and test cricket, but there has been a big crossover in time-wasting tactics.

As it happens, there are enough box office negatives built into the game without the antics of these serial saboteurs, and the failure of cricket to penetrate the North American market is evidence of this. One immediate stumbling block is the language. It is hard to explain to an American that the wicket is the playing surface. And the stumps? That's the wicket too. And when someone gets out? That's also a wicket. Whenever there is a chance to update and use the Australian terminology—pitch, stumps, dismissal—the chance is never taken. Try further explaining to an American that the whole field is called the pitch in England, and the 22-yard strip in the middle is also the pitch, as is the length of a delivery.

In the Broadway musical *How to Succeed in Business Without Really Trying*, the hero, J. Pierpont Finch, starts out as a window cleaner for the World Wide Wicket Company. The central joke of the piece is that Finchy works his way up to chief executive officer without knowing what a wicket is. The writers wanted a name for the company's product that would be faintly familiar but massively obscure and hard to explain, so what else would they hit on but wicket? For an American audience, it was perfectly pitched.

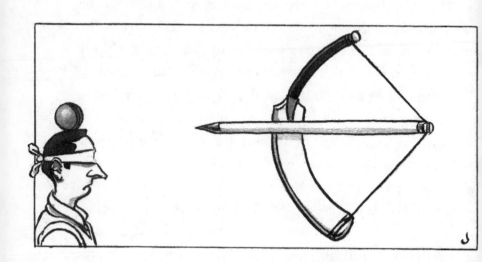

12

Wiping out Chux

Throw, throw, throw the ball
Gently in the air
Murali, Murali, Murali
Where is Darrell Hair?

song sung by the Barmy Army in Sri Lanka

Patrick Smith wrote in his column about Australian umpires like Darrell Hair: 'they had the courage to call Muttiah Muralitharan for his blatant throwing' (the *Australian*, 9 December 2003). This took considerable magnanimity on Smith's part. Not just a bearded face, he was a first-grade fast bowler for Prahran who was never picked to play for Victoria because it was said he was a chucker. Since 1958, throwing has been the controversy that just won't go to bed.

In the third Ashes test at Sydney in January 1959, there appeared the following line in the scorecard from the second innings: P.B.H. May, bowled Burke 92.

The English captain was one of the best batsmen of the postwar era, with a flawless technique, a proven big-match temperament, and the ability to dismember any substandard attack with his footwork and severe driving on both sides of the wicket. Jim Burke was a dour opening bat and very much a part-time bowler of off-breaks. May had no trouble with Ian Johnson, a full-time offie, in previous encounters both in Australia and England, and destroyed the West Indian spin twins Ramadhin and Valentine in the 1957 home series. The question remained: how on earth could a great batsman with no weaknesses get bowled when well set by a trundler bowling off-breaks on a good Australian pitch? There was only one possible explanation. Burke was a chucker, and the above scoreline was pretty close to being proof. The ball that bowled Peter May was suddenly a lot quicker than previous deliveries and jagged back to beat a man who was about to bring up yet another century against Australia. May was a fully paid up member of the Reflexes Mafia—those batsmen and fielders who react much more quickly than mere mortals and get selected for test cricket for this reason—but even he was not quick enough to keep out this ostensible off-break, which was a doozy rather than a doosra. Perfectly mannered, as always, May did not show dissent or even disappointment; he showed amazement.

The major wicket-takers in the Australian team were Richie Benaud and Alan Davidson, who were above suspicion with their flowing, classic actions. Benaud was a leg-spinner and, as we think we know, it is impossible to bowl a leg-break with anything other than a straight arm. Davo was a left-armer who was pure text-book in both run-up and delivery, like Larwood seen in a mirror. There were two other suspected chuckers in the Australian team for that test, Ian Meckiff and Keith Slater, but they were pace bowlers with whippy actions and their arms came over so quickly it was difficult to see any irregularity with the naked eye. From side-on, seen from the old Bob Stand, they just looked like normal bowlers, except that it was a mild surprise to see such pace from Meckiff after his ambling, unathletic run-up. No one in the crowd called 'no ball' or any of the other nonsense that was later to dog Muralitharan. Slater was a Sand-groper who did not have a long career, but Meckiff had a productive stint at home in winning series against England in 1958–59 and the West Indies in 1960–61. He was not selected for England in 1961 after South African Geoff Griffin had been no-balled for throwing during the previous season, and the tour proceeded without any scandals. Meckiff was finally no-balled out of test cricket by umpire Col Egar in the Brisbane test against South

Africa in December 1963. Victoria then embarked on a policy of not picking suspected chuckers for the state team, and only one bowler, Eddie Illingworth, subsequently slipped through the net and was called for throwing in a Sheffield Shield match. As for Jim Burke, he retired from test cricket in 1959, became a respected commentator for the ABC, and then took his own wicket in the idyllic Sydney suburb of Manly in early 1979.

'He'll take a thousand wickets, Murali,' said Shane Warne in Colombo in 2004, laughing at any suggestion that he, 'the Comeback Kid', would end up with more, or that it would even be a contest. Murali himself predicted after he took his 500th test wicket that he would probably break 600, despite having an action that looked like someone tossing a snake out the back door. Called for throwing only by Australian umpires, the Sri Lankan had added a mystery ball, the doosra, to his repertoire, and confounded the experts who said chuckers could not move the ball away from a right-handed batsman. After all, it had been an article of faith that Bill Lawry and 'Wallaby' Bob Cowper had been better able to cope with the blatant throwing of Charlie Griffiths in the West Indies in 1965 because they were left-handers and the ball moved away from their stumps because, it was said, chuckers can't bowl outswingers or leg-breaks (to right-handed batsmen) . . .

Another subcontinental bowler, Shoaib Akhtar, was said to look like a film star, so what did umpire Ross Emerson do? He filmed him. In a scarcely believable sequence of events that certainly fuelled Pakistani paranoia about Australia, Emerson took stress leave from the Perth police to stand as an umpire in international cricket matches. This concept of umpiring as some kind of haven from stress occasioned some satirical remarks about Western Australian work practices, but it was nothing compared to what happened next. Convinced that the much-bruited Akhtar was a chucker, but aware that this was not easy to see from square leg with a bowler of this extreme pace, Emerson filmed 'the Rawalpindi Express' from behind his arm in a tour game and then sent the results to the Australian Cricket Board. Incredibly, he also went public about what he had done.

The Pakistanis were furious, Akhtar was ropable, and the ACB was forced to say it had not seen the film, and that its auteur, although an accredited umpire (up to date), had not been asked to make or submit a film proving or disproving that that the Pakistani speedster bent his arm when bowling his faster deliveries. An academic from the University of Western Australia then tried to calm things down by issuing the diplomatic statement of the decade: 'Shoaib Akhtar has a uniquely flexible right arm.' As it turned out, Akka was later advised by the international board to take some time out to fix his action, and was then pronounced fit to resume his career. Some saw that as a victory for the growing power of the subcontinent in world cricket rather than as a Solomon-like judicial solution, but then others pointed out that Brett Lee 'flicked' his faster deliveries, too, and he had gone unpunished. As for the enterprising Emerson, his careers in umpiring and film-making were at an end, and there were no offers to join the diplomatic service or the Australia–Pakistan Friendship Society. To cap it all off, the Perth police were rated the worst in Australia in an impartial survey. Emerson had been the second umpire, after Darrell Hair in Melbourne in 1995, to call Murali for throwing, and had obviously developed a taste for blood, but it was never to be satisfied again. He did retain one 'first', however; he was the first umpire to stand in an international cricket match while on stress leave, and looks likely to be the only one ever to do so. For Emmo, who was labelled a 'nincompoop' by the *Sydney Morning Herald*, this bizarre record remains a souvenir of that memorable summer when he put on his very own Tropfest.

There have been many bowlers with peculiar actions that have offended against the aesthetics of cricket without actually being chuckers. Chris Harris, the underthatched Kiwi, bowls with an action so side-on he appears to be appealing to the square leg umpire before he releases the ball with his fan-like wrist movement. In a brilliant piece of commentary, Mark Taylor described Harris's deliveries as 'doorknobs', as he looks to be opening a door instead of bowling a cricket ball. Bhagwat Chandrasekhar took 242 test wickets for India bowling leg-breaks with a right arm that was withered by polio. He brought this skinny limb over so quickly—not much air resistance, perhaps— that it was impossible to tell with the naked eye whether he threw or not. He was exonerated by film—official film, that is—and was never called in his long career. Max 'Tangles' Walker and South African Mike Procter had nightmare actions, and could never have been held up as textbook examples or aesthetic ideals in the flowing, balanced mode of Larwood, Lindwall and Davidson. Walker bowled off the wrong foot and Procter's arm appeared to rotate independently of his body, but there was no suggestion of a bent elbow in either case.

Throwing is the ultimate offence against both fair play and the aesthetics of the game, but it is so difficult to detect with the naked eye that the usual procedure is for umpires to report any suspicions to the match referee and then for him to contact the International Cricket Conference for a 'screen test' of the bowler in question. In Australia, three umpires—Darrell Hair, Ross Emerson and Tony McQuillan—have chosen not to go down this road and have called Muttiah Muralitharan for throwing. Adam Gilchrist inadvertently let slip on a television sports comedy show that he thought Muralitharan was a chucker, and Brian Taylor said on Foxsports: 'He clearly chucks it. Ask any cricketer out of the public arena.' Finally, match referee Chris Broad said after the third test against Australia in 2004 that the doosra was a suspect delivery and Murali should have some films made of it. What does 'the Mural' think of all this? He asked to be excused from the next tour of Australia.

ARTHUR MAILEY

13

Scoundrel time

'That was a good yorker. Why do they call that kind of
   ball a yorker, Richie?'
'Well, what else would you call it?'

from *Inside Cricket*, Neil Evans

Not every cricketer has grown old and venerable before
our very eyes like 'the Sage of Coogee', Richie Benaud,
who is not now nor has ever been at a loss for an answer
to any of the major or minor questions thrown up by life.
It is remarkable, however, that so few ex-players have
gotten themselves into trouble, given the focus on bad
behaviour and dubious achievements and practices 'in the
press and the media generally', as Rex Mossop used to say.

The two 'bad boys' of the postwar era, Roy Gilchrist
and Vinoo Mankad, are now dead, but the devices they

invented or popularised, the beamer and the run-out of the non-striker, can still be seen, albeit more often in social or country cricket. It is a minor irony that the baddest dude of all, the West Indian fast bowler Gilchrist, shares the same name as the only Australian to walk, all-round good guy Adam Gilchrist. Big Roy was sent home from the West Indian tour of the subcontinent in 1959 for bowling beamers—full tosses directed at the batsman's head, or 'bench-emptiers', as they say in baseball—and missed out on participating in the only cricket match seen by a US president. Dwight D. 'Ike' Eisenhower was the guest of Pakistan strongman General Ayub Khan at the Karachi test against the West Indies in 1959, and contrary to popular belief did not say at five o'clock, 'This is great, but when are they going to start?' Ike and the general in fact left for an official lunch after the morning session, and Roy Gilchrist ended up in jail. 'If only he had gone to Boys' Town,' lamented a former Jamaican prime minister, Michael Manley.

Australia's postwar 'bad boy', Sid Barnes, went into premature retirement after his Adelaide Oval twelfth man comedy fiasco, and became a journalist, famously saying to Neville Cardus in the press box at a test match, 'Why don't we have alternate days off and use each other's material, Nev? After all, we both write the same sort of stuff.' Along with Jim Burke and Jack Iverson, Barnes took his own life in the 1970s, which apparently was a pretty depressing decade for ex-cricketers.

Another casualty of the 1970s was dashing, moustachioed spin bowler Leslie 'Chuck' Fleetwood-Smith, who did not 'chuck' and put in the 'Fleetwood' just for effect. Originally plain old Les Smith, this roué and sometime seducer of titled Englishwomen was a left-arm wrist-spinner who actually used to sledge his own team-mate, calling out 'Gee up, Bessie' whenever Bill O'Reilly ran in to bowl. A Celt, a Catholic a big drinker, the matinee idol Chuck went ll in the 1960s and became a derelict, sleepir gh along Punt Road not far from the MCG. F a been an expensive bowler, with a test average 38 per wicket, and had lived high on the hog, bu s a sad moment for his many friends and colleag nen he was found dead in 1971.

Ian M iff emerged as the most controversial Australian bowler of all time when he took 6 for 38 against England at the MCG in the second test of the 1958–59 series. Fleet Street went crazy, branding him a chucker and demanding he be sacked forthwith. E.M. Wellings of the *Evening Standard* wanted him banned for life, along with other alleged slingers Burke, Slater and Gordon Rorke, but Wello said nothing about Tony Lock. Meckiff had another five years in big cricket until he was no-balled out of the game and later sued former team-mate Bobby Simpson for calling him a chucker in his book *Captain's Story*. He went on to a comfortable career selling advertising space in cricket grounds—such as the MCG—when all the pointers suggested an embittered life away from sport.

Terry Jenner and Tony Lock were both prime candidates for the Eric Hollies Award, being forever linked to the better known Ashley Mallett and Jim Laker, but they had their moments on the field and generated much more scandal off it than their spin twins ever did. Jenner was a popular cricketer who only played nine tests before going into business. He had a gambling addiction and ran up debts that he felt could only be paid by embezzling money from his Adelaide firm and predictably ended up in jail, where he was faithfully visited by his former test and state skipper Ian Chappell. Lock had to wear the tag 'the only English chucker' and took two years out of test cricket to modify his left-arm finger-spinners, particularly a 'faster ball' that looked very jerky indeed. A whole hearted captain and mentor of Western Australia in his mature years, he also had to wear charges of molesting an under-age girl in Perth. The charges were dropped by the prosecution in 1994 just before Lock's premature death from cancer at the age of 65.

The night before a press conference in late 2003 Shane Warne's mother gave him a diuretic that she said would drain some of the water from his body and make him look slimmer for the cameras. The trouble is, diuretics are masking agents for steroids and are a banned substance. Did the quick recovery of Warne from a shoulder injury get some chemical help? wondered Tony Greig, but the question was never answered. Warney was banned for a year, but the drugs scandal faded as soon as it broke that the blond tweaker had approached a South African woman for sex, using as an opening gambit: 'You've got a nice-looking arse.' Coach David Hookes then took the heat when he questioned the credentials of 'some dopey hairy-backed sheila'. There was an avalanche of criticism for Hookesy along the lines of racism and sexism, and the media was kept busy for days. As an example of taking the scandal on the scandal and for sheer teamwork, this sequence had no peer in the serpentine path of cricket history.

Accused of displaying bad table manners in Sharjah ('How could they tell?' was no defence), balding off-spinner Greg Matthews was dropped from the Australian team but went on playing for New South Wales openly wearing a rug and doing commercials for a 'hair studio'. He remained on the outer with selectors, partly because of the paucity of test match wickets in his record, and partly, according to the *Australian*'s Malcolm Conn, because he had collaborated in the writing of 'an un-principled book'. This was *Calypso Cricket*, by Roland Fishman, an account of a tour to the West Indies, in which Matthews looms large—understandably, as Fishy was his friend and best-selling biographer. Despite its misleading cornball title (calypso music and calypso cricket died out in the 1960s), the book is both hilarious and indispensable, and is the kind of thing Woody Allen could have written if he had the talent. Journalists and other busybodies are called 'coats' by cricketers, and they are able to warn team-mates in code simply by fingering an imaginary lapel if a 'coat' hoves into view. This is simply one instance of Fishman's folklore scholarship in the book, but it was self-fulfilling if Matthews suffered setbacks because he associated with a 'coat' who went on to write 'an unprincipled book'. Why was *Calypso Cricket* rubbished thus? Well, a couple of paragraphs in its 297-page length dealt with un-named married players picking up girls in a bar and this was a violation of the Mates Act. A genuine innocent with a gift for screwing up, Fishy once missed—not dropped, missed—a simple catch in the annual Authors v. Publishers cricket match. It was the last ball and the batsmen—one of whom specialised in remainders and pulping—ran two to win the match for the Publishers by one run.

Greg Matthews was a colourful character who was badly injured in a Perth nightclub incident and declared persona non grata at Grace Bros Bondi Junction store after firing a cap gun at a sales clerk, but there are some who say he was simply a good state player whose off-breaks lacked penetration at test level. In this respect he is not Robinson Crusoe among Australian offies, and some keen judges said it was a pity he could not hang on until the 2000s, when world cricket came down to Pura Cup standards. What happened to the *Calypso* author Roly Fishman, who once said, 'I try to avoid clichés like the plague'? He became a creative writing teacher.

During a one-day match between Sri Lanka and England at Adelaide Oval, the wristy, elbowy, shouldery poster-boy Muttiah Muralitharan was called for throwing. Sri Lankan captain Arjuna Ranatunga sprang to the defence of the Mural, saying he did not throw and asking for the call to be withdrawn. Getting no satisfaction, Arjie led his team off the field and then, incredibly, and despite the time difference, rang the cricket board in Colombo to ask for instructions. They told him to get on with the game, and he did. What does 'Runner' Tunga do now? Well, with that record, what else? He became a politician, and has prospered mightily. When a slimline Shane Warne saw him in Sri Lanka in 2004 he said, 'You look as if you've swallowed a sheep.' A master of repartee, Ranatunga then revealed he had replied to his old adversary, 'At least I don't swallow everything my mother tells me to.'

Indian all-rounders are comparatively rare, but Manoj Prabhakar managed to be one both during and after his career. A scowling 'bad boy' who batted a little, bowled fast-medium and appealed a lot, MP toured Australia in

1991–92, where he made few friends but entertained people with his on-field antics. After retiring from cricket he became a whistleblower and fingered several colleagues—Azharuddin, Kapil Dev—as match-fixing scoundrels and throwers of games and generally murky characters with underworld connections. The investigations then moved to Prabhakar himself and he was accused of being a match-fixer. This triple—'bad boy', whistleblower, taker of dives and money—was unique, and not just in India. Manoj Prabhakar can lay claim to being the most versatile all-rounder the game has produced.

14

Water boys

Who urinated on the city gate of Melbourne?

from the German translation of
The Birthday Party, Harold Pinter

Before pitches were covered, the philosophy of cricketers
was 'What ho, she blows' and test matches would have
ludicrous innings scores like 9 for 32 (dec.) after a deluge.
Americans thought the expression 'a sticky wicket' was
hilarious, and it was the fashion for a long time, even after
pitches were covered, for upper-crust limeys to say in
American screenplays 'Bit of a sticky wicket, what?'
Batting on a 'sticky' was one of the game's arts and Victor
Trumper used to ask the SCG groundsman to water the
pitch at practice so he could get used to it and perfect
his armoury of strokes in these adverse conditions. None
of the other batsmen wanted to be seen floundering in

front of the selectors, so Trumper had an extended session. When the next wet pitch came along in Sheffield Shield and batsmen floundered, he often carried his bat or made a century and ensured his test place would continue to be a sinecure.

'Who watered the wicket at Melbourne?' became a famous unanswered question after the rest day in the Ashes series of 1954–55. It was asked again in Harold Pinter's 1957 play *The Birthday Party*, and emerged as 'Who urinated on the city gate of Melbourne?' in the German translation. Martin Esslin, who translated Pinter's later plays more accurately, told me the story and I was able to assure him that Melbourne was not in fact a gated community, however metaphorically it resembled one.

Melbourne Sundays of the 1950s were notoriously funereal, with empty streets, closed shops and nowhere to go for food or drink. It was easy to film location shots for *On the Beach*, Neville Shute's 1959 nuclear war fantasy in which everyone in the world dies, Melburnians ironically being the last to go. Cricket in this era had none of today's showbiz flair and in 1954–55 there was no convention that batsmen crossed on the field after a dismissal, no minimum overs in a day, no time made up after rain, no ground announcements and no acknowl-edgement whatsoever of the paying customer. There was also no Sunday play—forgoing the best gate—so that if a test match was building to a climax on the Saturday, they pulled up stumps at 6.00 p.m. no matter what and did not resume until Monday morning when everyone was at work and handclaps echoed in the stands.

During the Melbourne test in 1954–55 the heat was freakish and large cracks in the pitch opened up on the Saturday. When the players took the field on Monday morning the cracks had closed. Someone had watered the pitch during the rest day on Sunday—against the rules and playing conditions that the curator had to prepare a pitch that would last six days and the only maintenance was to be sweeping, re-marking the creases or sparing use of the roller under the direction of the captains. No miscreant was found, but quite obviously someone on the ground staff at the MCG was worried the match would be abandoned because of the large and dangerous cracks and that he would be accused of not doing his preparation properly. A possible defence—'I didn't know there was going to be a heatwave, Your Honour'—loomed as inadequate ('Ve don't do meteorology here!'), so the fearful groundie took to the pitch with a watering can and it played beautifully, much better than the normal MCG square, for the remainder of the match (which England won; when they doctor pitches in England they win there, too).

In dry countries like Zimbabwe, it is often the (illegal) custom to water a pitch early on the morning of a day's play, especially if it is known that the visiting team will be batting. According to former test player John Traicos, this process, known as 'freshening up', rebounds on the fresheners-up as often as it helps them. This did not happen in Australia's second most notorious case of 'unwanted shale attention', which also happened in Melbourne.

Fourteen years after the Mystery of the Watered Wicket came the semi-finals of the district competition (first grade) in 1968–69. The match between Carlton and the University of Melbourne was played at Princes Park on 15 and 16 March 1969. The students did not 'Beware the Ides of March' and ended up paying the penalty.

Carlton batted on the Saturday and only made 136, a total which the strong University batting side, which included test player Paul Sheahan, believed they would have no trouble passing on the Sunday. When they got to the ground on the fateful day they discovered that someone had placed a block of ice on a good length and that it had slowly melted overnight, leaving a damp patch that bowlers used to dream about. Although Paul Sheahan made 29 Trumper-style runs, no one else reached double figures and the University boys were routed for 62, with the ball doing crazy things, seaming and propping and sliding off the affected area. Only two bowlers were used, Barry Knight, who took 7 for 20, and Barney Jones, father of Deano, who backed up the England all-rounder with 3 for 36.

The newspapers went for their usual 'The Iceman Cometh' headlines; the O'Neill play was at this stage 23 years old and, as has been noted, had never been produced in Australia. Who was the Iceman? Some people fingered Barney Jones, but that could involve a kind of reverse lineage factor. Suspects included Percy Jones, a former Carlton footballer and coach who owned a local hotel, and Adrian Gallagher, a Carlton cricketer—or was it both of them? Another Blues identity, Wes Lofts, was allegedly involved, as he was supposed to have bet on the double— Carlton for both the VFL and the VCA premierships. As the Blues had already won the 1968 flag, defeating Essendon 56–53 on a wet ground, Wes Lofts was looking good. As with the earlier scandal, however, nothing was proved, and in 2002, when Carlton met University in a special game for the Ice Block Cup, investigations could be said to have reached a stalemate.

The use of a block of ice has only one precedent in Brisbane cricket and it was a New South Welshperson, or 'Cockroach', who was the perp. During the first test in Brisbane in 1946 there was a subtropical storm, with hailstones the size of golf or tennis balls, depending on which report you believed. Seeing the English team peering out of their dressing room window with some alarm at this exotic monsoonal onslaught, Sid Barnes decided to take a block of ice out of the icebox (it was Brisbane, 1946) and really give them a fright. He opened the door to their dressing room, threw in the ice block and then enjoyed the hoots and hollers that ensued.

The phenomenon of 'horizontal rain' was taken more seriously in the semi-final of the Sydney Cricket Association first-grade premiership in March–April 2002. Drummoyne Oval was the home ground of one of the contestants, UTS–Balmain, and when the teams arrived on the second day of this dry Sydney autumn, with North Sydney only needing 50 to win, they discovered that the pitch was mysteriously damp, despite covers and no dew, let alone rain. Norths, who had not won the premiership since 1935, refused to play on, the home side claimed a forfeit and legal action ensued. The chairman of the SCA, Bruce Collins QC, ruled that the teams should play their second day on the Friday of the following week at Bankstown Oval, and then the final should begin the next day. 'It's our aim,' he said, 'to make sure we do the fairest thing possible for both teams and to make sure it's played out on the field rather than in the protest room.'

And so it happened that on the Friday at Bankstown Oval North Sydney duly won their semi-final and then on the weekend were easily beaten by jubilant first-time premiers Fairfield–Liverpool. David Sygall commented on Sunday of that weekend in the *Sun-Herald*: 'The North Sydney players looked tired after spending hours in the field yesterday, having earned the right to contest the final less than 24 hours before it started.'

Supporters of the North Sydney rugby league team remember when a home ground football match was called off because of local flooding and club secretary Harry 'Akka' Forbes announced to the press, 'The game has been cancelled due to a delugg.'

This introduction of 'horizontal rain' to thwart a straightforward victory and prevent a week of preparation for the final was a cruel blow to the cricketing arm of the proud North Sydney fraternity and would not have dampened traditional speculation that 'they'll do anything to beat us'. For Norths, the premiership drought reached its sixty-seventh year.

15

The Eric Hollies award

When it comes to fame, it's still a batsman's game.

Traditional (attributed to Eric Hollies)

Don Bradman's last test innings at the Oval in 1948 would not have been possible without the usual support staff: 21 other players and two umpires. The Don was bowled for a duck by leg-spinner Eric Hollies, while at the other end Arthur Morris was compiling a massive and largely unnoticed 196. Who wins the Eric Hollies award for neglected effort? That's right, Arthur Morris. Poor old Eric never backed a winner on his birthday.

In the 2003 World Cup final, Harbhajan Singh made a clean sweep of the Australian wickets and took out the Eric Hollies award. How could that be possible? Well, you see, Australia made 359 for the loss of only two wickets and Harbhajan's contribution went almost completely unnoticed. This is the prime requisite for the prize, which, as you may have gathered, is an imaginary one—although none the less valuable for that, it is to be hoped.

Don Bradman had everything to live for on that overcast but dry day at the Oval in 1948. He only needed to score four runs to be the first batsman in history to go into the third column and end up with a test average of 100. There was a 'good crowd in' and English skipper Norman Yardley had just called for three cheers to honour the mighty Don. Why, then, did he depart soon after with a second-ball duck to his name? It was, in fact, a very good delivery from Eric Hollies: it was a perfectly pitched wrong 'un that went through the gate, it was dead on the stumps and it took the wicket of the batsman with the best technique the world had ever seen. It was right up there with Gatting bowled Warne in 1993 and Hughes bowled Qadir in 1984 and the daddy of them all, Wasim Akram's two devastating—if tarnished—dismissals in the 1992 World Cup final. Yet while some of these milestones are endlessly replayed and praised to the skies, Hollies is hardly ever mentioned and his achievement has been downgraded and ignored. At best, he is seen as a party-pooper or a spectre at the feast.

In narrating a television documentary on 100 years of test cricket, the florid John Arlott asked rhetorically: 'Who could have thought that Don Bradman would be beaten

and bowled by Eric Hollies' little googly? Was the mighty
Don's eagle eye dimmed by a tear?' Unbelievable! A classic
delivery is demeaned as a 'little googly', and that feeble
excuse that the unsentimental 'Braddles', he of the cold
heart and hot mind, was too tearful to see the ball properly is simply too ridiculous for words. No wonder some
people put an apostrophe in front and called the man
'Arlott! The expression 'googly' was replaced some years
ago by 'wrong 'un', so JA has revealed himself as both a
fuddy-duddy and a cog in the Bradolatry machine. Of all
the bad behaviour in sport that is criticised by fan and
commentator alike, surely this kind of elitism, this
rubbishing of an honest journeyman, this overlooking of
a stalwart pro, is the worst kind of crass bad manners and
could even be tagged as incipient fascism. It is also not
very nice.

In every walk of life and in most institutions there will
be an Eric Hollies, but in cricket the biggest Eric Hollies
was the man himself. There were, however, some interesting placegetters.

When Don Bradman walked out to bat in the second
test at Melbourne in 1932 it was his first appearance in
the series. He was applauded all the way to the crease,
took block and was promptly bowled first ball by Bill
Bowes, a tall Yorkshireman in glasses who looked like a
popular chemistry teacher. It was the only wicket Bowes
took in this notorious Bodyline series and once again the

coverage was all Bradman, with the bowler reduced to being, well, an Eric Hollies figure. Bradman had been bowled for a duck in a 1930 Sheffield Shield game by Queenslander Eddie Gilbert, but this reedy lightning-fast Aborigine did not go further in the game and by the end of the decade had been institutionalised for mental disorders.

The curse of elitism has blighted many careers, but the match-saving 36 scored by John Watkins at Sydney against Pakistan in 1973 had the distinction of being overshadowed by his own performance with the ball. Overcome by nerves, Wock bowled a record number of wides in this, his only test, and as a result only a few wizened buffs remember his defiant innings that kept Australia in the game so Max Walker could perform his heroics with the ball (6 for 15) and deny Pakistan their first win away from home against the 'new enemy'.

Unlike poor old 'Wock' Watkins, with his 'Jeckyll and Wide' problems, Hans Ebeling was an effortless Eric Hollies award-winner, appearing in only one test for Australia, at the Oval in 1934, where he took a more than respectable 3 for 89 with his swinging fasties and made 41 with the bat. It was a 'sparkling debut', as they would say on Channel Nine, but it went unnoticed and Ebeling became even less famous than Eric Hollies himself. A good Victorian, he was at the age of 72 a leading organiser for the Centenary Test at the MCG in 1977 and was actually interviewed on television. He came across as charming, highly articulate and with a full set of marbles, but once again fame did not come knocking.

Chetan Chauhan was not necessarily an Eric Hollies figure in his overall career, but the Indian opener was definitely cast in that role at the MCG in 1981 when his batting partner Sunil Gavaskar was given out—wrongly, in the batsman's view. No fan of Australian umpiring, a livid Sunny asked Chauhan to accompany him off the field in some kind of boycott or 'match abandoned' tactic, and CC actually agreed. Off they went, heading towards an incendiary scandal and a potentially unsolvable problem. Of course, when the odd couple reached the players' gate, Chauhan was ordered to go back to the crease by a furious team manager and did in fact resume his innings, but those few minutes of walking the walk with friend Gavaskar, that journey to the boundary as a non-striker going out in sympathy, that moment of agreement with the man who had been given out . . . that was the stuff that Eric Hollies awards are made of.

That most astute of film critics, Rob Lowing, said when reviewing *The Quiet American*, 'characters-as-countries symbolism does not work for a modern audience', and there is no doubt she was right, but there was something about John Emburey that was very English, very county cricket English, very much the economical pro playing for a draw, a symbol of the muzzled bulldog breed, that meant the Lowing decree would have to be suspended or at least rewritten when applied to sport. Was Embers an off-spinner? Was he a box office saboteur? How could he have been anything other than both? To see him bowling tightly to a packed leg-side field under the captaincy of Mike Brearley in the Packer-ravaged Australia of 1978–79 was not something that the cricketing public can recall with affection or even recall, which is very Eric Hollies award.

Albert Padmore became a name to conjure with for those with an interest in the legacy of Eric Hollies. The three-pronged West Indian spin attack in that watershed Port of Spain test in 1976 consisted of Raphick Jumadeen, Imtiaz Ali and Albert Padmore. Fate never had more capable lieutenants than these three, who did the Eric Hollies thing and unwittingly ended an era. The story has often been told of how India made 4 for 406 to win the test and that Clive Lloyd henceforth decreed that pace was the answer and the West Indies would be a no-spin zone. 'How many runs would you have needed?' enquired a caustic Lloyd of his spin trio in the dressing room afterwards. India's batsmen are the best players of spin in the world, and Albert Padmore could have pointed out that they were just too good on the day ('Full credit to the boys . . . '). It would be wrong to blame Albert Padmore for the broken bones, slow over rates and empty seats that accompanied the West Indian pace era, but it would be so right to recommend him for an Eric Hollies award, for the world has largely forgotten Albert Padmore.

When Suicide took his Michelle in Galle, who won the Hollies? Say what??? To explain a bit further . . . taking five wickets, or five-fer, is sometimes called a 'Michelle', as in Michelle Pfeiffer, the very attractive film star. In the first test at Galle, Sri Lanka, in 2004, Shane Warne, the suicide blond, took 5 for 43 in the second innings, including his 500th test wicket when Andrew Symonds took a catch to dismiss Hashan Tillekeratne. Symonds is indisputably the Eric Hollies figure here as Tillers is not only the captain of his team, but he was Warney's 500th victim and he'll always have Galle. No one will remember how he got out or who took the catch, but there is no reason to believe that explosive test debutant Andrew Symonds will go on to have an Eric Hollies-style career. Ken Eastwood wrote the book on that.

For the unprecedented seventh test of the 1970–71 Ashes series, Australian captain Bill Lawry was dropped—because, it was said, of his slow scoring and negative tactics. His replacement was a good Victorian, Ken Eastwood, who scored 5 and 0, and took 1 for 21 with his slows. Easty never played in another test and fulfilled all the requirements for an Eric Hollies fellowship, if they had existed at the time. He could have joined a short-lived South Australian premier, Des Corcoran, who succeeded Don Dunstan and then called an early election, and 1970s New Zealand Davis Cup player Onny Parun on a lecture tour called 'Fame and Western Man' with Martha Hyer, that perennial supporting player, as the chair/compere. Who is to say it would not have been a success?

Wayne Daniel was a West Indian fast bowler who was partly to blame for the notorious underarm incident of 1981, but it was Mick Malone who picked up the Eric Hollies award. Perhaps I had better explain.

At the end of a one-day international against Australia in 1980, the West Indies needed six to win off the last ball of the match. Wayne Daniel was the batsman and the setting was the vast MCG. Mick Malone was the bowler and no one thought a tail-ender like Daniel had a hope in hell of bringing off a victory. Just to be safe, though, Malone bowled the traditional—in these circumstances— inswinging yorker. It was fractionally short and strayed fractionally outside leg stump and Daniel backed away towards square leg and swung the bat in a big arc. Bango! He connected and the ball sailed away for six. In the West Indies dressing room pandemonium broke out. They were jumping for joy and almost ignoring a beautiful blonde in a red dress, who was struggling to get out the door and no doubt reward those who needed rewarding. Who was the Woman in Red? She was never identified publicly, but there is no need to finger the winner of the Eric

Hollies award. Mick Malone was the obvious choice. One year later, New Zealand needed six off the last delivery to win and Greg Chappell instructed his brother Trevor to bowl it underarm so there would be no more sixes and, as a bonus, the skipper's contempt for the MCG pitch and the playing schedule would also be expressed. There was no sign of the Woman in Red on that day. This rather confirmed the view that the West Indians had turned Australia into a kind of reverse Tahiti as far as women were concerned, that these black men had happened on an island of pliable whites, the opposite of what befell the crew of the *Bounty*. Indeed, a skippy chick once asked the six-feet-eight Joel Garner if everything was in proportion and received the predictable reply: 'No. If it was, I'd be nine feet tall.'

Eric Hollies was a genuine rabbit with the bat and never looked like hitting a six, or indeed a single. Like Bill Bowes, he had a record that showed a greater number of wickets taken than runs scored. Terry Jenner was not like that, and saved Australia in the Adelaide test of the 1974–75 Ashes series with a well-made 74. He was dropped from the test team for his efforts in a classic Eric Hollies award-winning performance. Four years earlier he had won another Hollies when John Snow hit him on the head with a bouncer and knocked him down, almost precipitating a riot. 'Bad boy' Snow and captain Ray Illing-worth ran away with all the headlines and photos, with their histrionics and threatened walk-offs (plus Snowy's broken hand), but it was Jenner who ended up with the award that Eric Hollies would have been proud to win. Metaphorically speaking, his fingerprints are all over it.

16

Would you like to buy twelve white jumpers?

Their bats are like the pitch in miniature.
Each one is badly scarred with the hot spots
And rashes of that disease which spreads beyond
The playing victims to their wives and kids—
The sempiternal* pain of a middle-order collapse.
But perhaps worse are those more personal wounds:
The split webbing after a dropped slips catch,
Two broken toes from practising in sandshoes,
And everyman's nightmare of turning full-on
To an awkward ball without the vital box.
When banishment from next week's team is likely
The anatiferous** number three will come back
To this uncovered nave*** and go through strokes
With all the devotion of a former sinner.

from *The Practice Nets*, Philip Hodgins

---

*   eternal, everlasting
**   of or pertaining to ducks
***   as in church (an 'uncovered knave' is a streaker)

There had been a shower of rain but it went away and the sun came out as if to say 'Just foxing!', so we resumed the game of cricket in Centennial Park, the 'lungs of Sydney'. I was bowling to a bookshop proprietor who had placed my autobiographical works on the fiction shelves, so I was keen to take his wicket. When he played a horrible cross-bat shot at a ball that was heading for off stump I was exultant for a split second. The ball duly hit the stump and then cannoned down towards third man. The batsmen ran three as I stared at the bails, willing just one of them to fall down, but they never did. The rain had washed out their varnish and the sun had glued them to the stumps. It was a real-life 'sticky wicket', but I spent little time marvelling at the phenomenon.

'Could you signal "stump byes", please?' I asked the umpire.

'How the hell can I do that?' he demanded. He was obviously new to social cricket, where the signalling is much more imaginative than in the professional game. I have seen an umpire successfully mime 'the ball hit a box of matches in his hip pocket' to a congregation about a hundred metres away. The keeper was not keen to have it down as byes and I would have rioted if it had been credited as runs, so the umpire eventually signalled leg byes. At the next drinks break—by which time the life-is-fiction man was on about 40—I explained what had happened to the scorer. He was most sympathetic and created a little window in the scorebook which read 'Stump Byes 3,'. I was not pleased to see the comma, which seemed to presage more of these horrors, but scorers in social games have to keep an open mind; anything can happen. Just the same, I had wiped those bails pretty thoroughly with a cloth between overs and, it has to be admitted, said something to the batsman along the lines of 'They'll drop off next time' [expurgated version].

Walking through what is now 'Centennial Parklands' on a rare day free of corporate marquees, I reflected that those of us who played there on the beautiful turf wickets in years gone by certainly had the best of it. The pitch at what we called Port of Spain is now a heel-bruiser—concrete overlaid with an artificial grass carpet—and the Canary Island date palms that made it look like our conception of the West Indies have gone, replaced by the dark leaves of the scrawny and slow-growing kauri pine. 'It's much nicer than the real Port of Spain,' said Peter Philpott, who toured there in 1965 and played in the Bodyline television series team against us at Cent Park in 1984, losing both times. When we played on the other turf pitch at the eastern or Bondi end of the park, called the Obelisk, a beautiful lady in a dented Saab occasionally stopped to watch, but now there are large and unromantic signs which read 'No Parking on Grassed Areas'. We called this ground the Obelisk because there was a small stone with a steel fence commemorating the swearing in of Australia's first federal government by Governor-General Hopetoun in 1901. When the ball hit the obelisk it was four runs, but there is no chance of that now. In 1988 a dome was built around it to give proper recognition to the historic site. It looks as if a World War I soldier has been buried vertically in full uniform, with birds nesting under the brim of the helmet. No longer a cricket ground, the rest of the green sward has been given over to dogs, which arrive in vans marked 'Walkies' or 'Dogue'.

Various levels of social cricket were played in the park, and some continue, albeit more sporadically than in the 1980s, when every venue was filled. There are the casual, or down-market types, who play in shorts or jeans, and they are distinguished usually by swaying umpires and a dog at third man. Those who play more seriously—and are called 'wanquers' by the smellysocks—are usually in long whites, with no bottles allowed on the field. What unites all forms of social cricket, from the black shirts to the white, is that there is no leg before wicket. If a batsman stands in front of the stumps and pads up, then you have to try to bowl him around his legs, giving new meaning to the leg-cutter, because the umpire—supplied by the batting side—will never give him out lbw. There are exceptions, of course. I once trapped a batsman plumb with three successive balls and the finger finally went up in answer to my hoarse appeal on the third. The umpire was, of course, immediately replaced, and I didn't look over to see how he was received when he got back to his team-mates. This is the code of conduct in social cricket; it is not Darwinian or Genghis Khanian, but you should not be surprised at anything.

In a charity game for Lord's Taverners on the Central Coast, it became clear who are the worst sledgers in any form of cricket: Hungarian-born boxers. Yes, Aussie Joe Bugner was one of the loudest mouths on a crowded field and no one was inclined to take issue with the demonic blond giant. Other players included tennis stars (John Alexander, Brad Drewett), television personalities Katrina Lee and Harry Potter [sic], politicians (John Howard), actors (Andrew Blackman), cricketers (Ross Edwards, Kim Fazackerly), rugby league and cricket stars (Graeme Hughes), jockeys (Mark de Montfort), journalists (Peter Fitzsimons), John Arlott impersonators (Mike Coward) and just one writer (er . . . moi).

I thought one of the highlights of the day came when I hit four successive boundaries off a future prime minister's off-spin bowling, but the ground announcer was quiet during this period of play, giving the lie to the 'leftist bias in the media' canard. Another revelation came when a husky batter from the Australian women's team and I bowled in tandem and shut the opposition down. We both tossed up the same sort of undistinguished stuff—medium

pace, reasonable length, doing a fraction off the seam—
and I thoroughly enjoyed bowling with someone who
could keep it tight at the other end. If only I'd eaten my
porridge and grown up bigger and stronger and then had
an operation . . . I could have walked into the women's
team. It is hard to feel triumphant about defeating a team
containing a heavyweight boxer and a pregnant news-
reader, but in social cricket a win is a win, and we felt
good afterwards. It was the warm genius of our captain
Graeme Hughes, a man of all sports, that kept the atmosphere competitive yet genial and the socialising afterwards
was all friendly, although John Howard said nothing to
me and I was never invited to Kirribilli House.

One of the more curious of the teams on the social
circuit—and there were some doozies (Plato's Curse,
Lenin's Eleven, PhoenIX XI, The Smiths, the Ten Past
Eleven, the Broadway Hits, the G.D. Barnard Invitation
XI, the Bondi Bystanders)—was the one that represented
a city hotel where resting actors gathered and English
crims sold stolen goods. One of the triumphs of Australia's
immigration policy is the almost complete importation
of London's underworld, two hundred years after it was
done for the first time. As a result you will never hear an
Australian accent selling scalped tickets outside sporting
venues; they are all Cockneys ('tickits!'). When we arrived
at the ground to play this hotel team, the captain came
over—to toss, I thought. 'You're the skipper?' he inquired,

and I said yes, for the day. He looked me up and down and then gazed into the middle distance and asked in a soft voice, 'Would you like to buy twelve white jumpers?'

JOCK ALEXANDER

17

Country practices

There's a standin' crop, an' the rain's not far,
An' the price is rotten, but there you are:
As soon as these cricketin' games begin
The farm goes dilly on listenin' in:
Not only the boys an' the harvester crew,
But Mum and the girls gits dotty too.
An' I reckon (said Dad) that a man's worst pests
Is this here wireless an' these here tests.

from *Dad on the Test*, C.J. Dennis

On the other side of the sandstone curtain, in 'rural and regional Australia', as the well-worn phrase has it, there are popularly supposed to be all sorts of colourful characters in cricket: bearded bushies, umpires with a wooden leg puffing on a pipe, and blokes bending the rules and behaving badly and wearing bizarre costumes on the field—top hats, jock straps and hobnail boots—just like the bad old days at the Bong Bong picnic races. Not so, say the people who play cricket in the country, none of that happens, although the Kookaburra Cricket Club concedes it does have an umpire with a wooden leg and a pipe.

The Kookas play at the Gundowringa Oval, outside Goulburn on the way to Crookwell and according to club stalwart Graeme Henson, they are no respecters of reputation. 'When Kerry O'Keefe bowled here, the first three went over the fence,' he relates. Did this continue? 'Well, no, he started to make some inroads, but country players tend not to get overawed.'

Cricket evangelist Jack Chegwyn used to tour New South Wales with a team of test and state players and there was an element of Jimmy Sharman's boxing troupe about the whole exercise, with local bowlers keen to roll up their sleeves and have a go at the big stars and maybe take a wicket or two. If someone got Neil Harvey out, for instance, it was worth a few beers, and gave rise to some anecdotes with legs.

Was there any sledging of Kerry O'Keefe at Gundowringa? Surely the hitting of three successive sixes would have occasioned some lively verbal banter. 'Well no, we didn't know him very well,' says Graeme Henson. 'Never sledge a stranger' appears to be a motto in the bush, where players are more inclined to abuse members of their own team than the opposition. 'Sledging in the country is based on familiarity,' explains Henson, 'and young blokes joining a club soon learn that.' When Sydney's fiery Len Pascoe bowled against a Kookaburra veteran he let fly with the same string of expletives every time he beat the bat, which was early and often. When he inevitably claimed the wicket, it was the batsman who supplied his own send-off: 'You may be a better cricketer than I am, Lenny, but I could sure as hell beat you at Scrabble.'

What about chucking? Are there any chuckers in the bush leagues? 'No,' says the long-time Kooka: 'A chucker would be found out by his team-mates and urged to change his action or become a specialist batsman.' The only chicanery bowlers will admit to is putting the ball in the freezer for a week so it would bounce like crazy, but even here justice prevailed; you had to do all the damage in the first hour because after that it became more like a blancmange.

When it comes to dress codes or gender-bending there are no takers for anything bizarre at Gundowringa. The teams are all male, all in white, all the time. There are no red socks and black braces, no Billy Jack hats or spotted Tootal ties wrapped around the mid-section. Ladies happily bring a plate and mingle at barbecues after the game, but you will not find any Zoe Gosses or Rachel

Heyhoe-Flints on the field. Generally speaking, the players follow the dictum laid down by John Birmingham in his book *How To Be a Man*: 'Only wear a Greek fisherman's cap if you're a Greek fisherman.'

The Kookaburras have gone on a tour of England and Graeme Henson fondly remembers three likely lads from Cobar, a small remote town known to more than one city-bred schoolteacher as 'Cobar the Dread'. Each day at breakfast on tour the triangular part of the lads' ties seemed to be hoist higher and higher until there was very little neckwear on view. Enquiries revealed that the Cobar boys did not know how to tie a tie and simply loosened them and lowered them over their heads every day.

There are no box office saboteurs in the country game, says Henson, 'Hanging around is not in their coaching manual. They attack the bowling from the word go.' It would be unusual for bush teams to suffer from the complacency neuroses known to city coaches as 'dead rubber syndrome' or 'the pipe and slippers complex'. Older fans remember the explosive entry of country legends Doug Walters (Digger Doug from Dungog) and the Sheikh of Burrell Creek, Johnnie Martin, into Sydney cricket. Walters is still credited with the longest six ever hit in the Moore Park area, a missile that was launched from SCG No. 2 and landed in Kippax Lake. The late John Wesley Martin, the man with a name like a Bob Dylan album, had forearms seemingly made of steel mesh and once terminated a ball at the SCG with such extreme prejudice that it landed in the Showground.

It was perplexing, therefore, to find on the Kookaburras' tour of England that opposing batsmen were defence-oriented and used unknown terms like 'a winning draw'. After three or four draws, the Kookas switched to a limited-over format so they could get some results. The pitches played low and slow—back in Crookwell the ground is 'as hard as a cat's head'—but once they started winning and losing the tour became more and more enjoyable.

When Armidale bowler Ray Blair took a hat-trick consisting of three leg before wickets in the local first-grade competition the statistically-minded started hunting through the record books. Three ell bees! Some bowlers have grumbled it is hard to get one a year in the bush, while others have drawn realistic conclusions about hard grounds and high bounce, as well as the incidence of bloodlines. As Campbell Alexander succinctly put it at the end of his wonderful tale of country cricket *The Beethoven Variations*:

Oberon Centrals 113 (R.Heller 4–28, J.Heller 5–62)
Lost to
Hazelgrove 2–116 (P.Heller 58, B.Heller 41*)

In this catch-22 or bowl-22 ambience you just know what the umpire's surname was.

ARTHUR MAILEY

M. A. Noble
Australia's greatest
captain

18

Flannelled Addisons

If you can't be a cricketer, at least look like one.

M.A. Noble to player wearing red socks at practice

If you can't be a drover, at least look like one.

from *The Sundowners*, Jon Cleary

According to Patrick Furlong, the 1977 Packer revolution was the most far-reaching of all the shocks cricket has suffered. The former head of ABC Sport lists the multi-camera set-ups for television, the commentary team made up exclusively of ex-players and the introduction of coloured clothing as the three big changes. It is of course the dress code that is the most immediately apparent. Of the beautifully creamed flannels and bristling moustaches of the Edwardian era, only the moustaches remained in the modern game. If you looked as if you were going to a barbecue or a pyjama party, then you looked like a cricketer. If you celebrated the centenary of Federation in 2001 by putting a blue rinse through your hair, as Colin 'Funky' Miller did, then you looked like nothing on earth. More than one spectator murmured, 'Thank God Alan McGilvray's not around to see this.' Is there any link between looking bad and bad behaviour? Does zero for Deportment always mean zero for Conduct? Nothing has been proven—yet.

The traditional elegance of the cricketer was embodied by the Edwardian test player C.B. Fry, who actually was a scholar and a gentleman, and always wore creams, not whites, a long-sleeved shirt, never one with short sleeves, and pleated trousers with a button fastener, never a belt or braces. Fry was famous for his aphorisms, such as 'Play back, or drive' and was the enemy of the push-and-prod school of batting. He looked like a Greek god, and was in fact offered the monarchy of Albania, but his rumoured reason for turning it down ('You can't get good help in Tirana these days') seems unlikely. The loose-fitting flannels of the day looked good on the tall, patrician figure of Fry, but did not suit the shorter, stockier journeymen like Charlie Macartney. In the 1960s the tighter fitting body shirt, pegged pleatless strides and ripple-soled look pioneered by John Benaud and John Snow caused apoplexy among the administrators, but now it seems ludicrous, like the clothes on *Get Smart* re-runs. At least everyone looked ludicrous, as befits a more democratic age. It had been Benaud the Elder who had opened the door in the 1950s by leaving his shirt unbuttoned at the top ('heroically slashed', said one scribe). This was frowned upon by conservative elements, the 'offended purists' of legend, but they had lots of bigger shocks in store, as cream gave way to white, and the picket fence began to disappear under the coloured tin hoardings advertising almost everything.

In the late 1950s, Arnold Palmer revolutionised golf with his casual clothing and Wichita lineman's swagger (also known as 'the perp walk'). He took golf out of its plus-fours and country-club image and made it popular right across the social spectrum; as soon as they saw him stumping down the fairway on television, increasingly followed by Arnie's Army, millions of men said instantly, 'I must buy myself some clubs'—it was that quick.

By the 1980s, Rodger Davis was getting on the television news because he was wearing plus-fours. In tennis, an American hacker called Trey Waltke wore long white trousers at Wimbledon and was dutifully covered by the television news. In an interview he was asked why he was doing this and he muttered something about being 'between sponsorships' and tried it out a 'just for fun'. The correct answer was 'So I can get on the television news.'

Harry Hopman was the first tennis player to wear shorts and when he appeared at White City in the 1930s, the reaction was so negative that for some time Hop was the only one in shorts. In his invaluable sports history book *Great Players of Australian Tennis*, Paul Metzler describes the reaction to Hopman's apostasy:

> There were mumblings in the giant old White City stand that he looked like someone who'd cut off his elder brother's long pants, and grumblings that that chap down there would look better on Bondi Beach, with a bucket and spade in his hand instead of a racquet. But Hopman was right, as always.

By 1945 no major player appeared in long trousers on a tennis court, and the complaints evaporated. The larrikin innovator Hopman later became famous again as Australia's Davis Cup (non-playing) captain, 1950–69, when he introduced fines for bad behaviour by the players and was known far and wide as a disciplinarian and arch conservative.

Sixty years after shorts made their debut in tennis, Dean Jones tried to introduce them to cricket, convincing his Victorian team-mates to turn out in what looked like longish white culottes for a state game. It made the television news, of course, and Deano scored an interview, but shorts looked horrible on a cricket oval and the whole idea was junked. By 2004 you had to be a woman or a transsexual playing in a men's tournament to get an interview on the television news; the interest in retro or avant-garde clothes had waned. Glancing through the cricket *Who's Who*, I noticed C.B. Fry was wearing a shirt with a snappy button-down collar in about 1905 and the awful thought occurred . . . did Seebs think that would get his photo into the papers? If so, he was right.

A further development in cricket apparel—the wearing of helmets—dates from the mid-1970s, but it was not a Packer innovation, as some have thought. It was Mike Brearley in 1975 who sported the first protective head-gear, a skullcap with a grey metallic tinge that he wore under his normal England cap and which sent out the message 'I have brains. They need protecting.' Then came Tony Greig in the Packer years with his motorcycle helmet that looked like one half of the cone of silence and had to be taken to the panel-beaters after a ping. From this developed the modern helmet with grill that was adopted by everyone except Viv Richards. The 'master blaster' thought they were sissy and he faced the quickest of the quicks wearing only his baggy maroon West Indies cap. In defence of those who did wear helmets, it has to be said they looked just as sick and spilt just as much blood after being pinged as they did before the revolution. They also looked like gladiators and carried out on to the field with them the idea that sport is war with rules.

It is only in the lesser forms of cricket that the full panoply of costumes through the ages can be seen. In the Authors teams, which set Sydney social cricket alight in the 1980s, Jon Cleary was a sterling example, wearing beautifully creamed flannels and white boots with pylon-style studs. He bowled well-flighted off-breaks and took heaps of wickets, but in a newspaper interview I described him as a 'pusher and a deflector' when it came to batting. JC then wrote a letter to the editor with the mock complaint that he thought he was a stylist, a 'flannelled Addison'* rather than a pusher and a deflector, and that my interview had been a blow to his amour-propre. It has to be said he certainly looked the part, unlike Tom Keneally, who played only once and turned out in cross-trainers, blue jeans and a Greek fisherman's cap. He made a first-ball duck and occasioned the enquiry: 'How can someone who writes so well and so knowledgeably about rugby league know so little about cricket?' The answer must be that God distributes his gifts evenly.

Cleary was one of many authors who have lifted lines from cricket and placed them in fiction. In *The Sundowners*, one of the characters on a cattle drive is a defrocked skipper from a boat plying the South China Sea. He still wears his old seafaring cap and provokes the comment: 'If you can't be a drover, at least look like one.'

---

* the essayist, not the disease man

Jon Cleary, the author of that cleverly transposed line, certainly looked like a cricketer, but he was close to being Robinson Crusoe.

Fellow novelist Barry Oakley, perhaps still smarting from the parental decision that landed him with the initials 'B.O.', wrote that the Authors team looked like 'a chain gang on day leave', and this was, it has to be conceded, a fair comment. From Louis Nowra's black shoes to Bob Ellis's 1961 corduroys—they may have been cream, but they were still intermittently corduroy—the costume parade was not inspiring. P.G. Wodehouse's fastidious character Psmith once said he stopped playing village cricket after being caught at point by a man wearing braces; luckily for Psmith's sensibilities, he never played on the Sydney Fringe.

As spectators we have now got used to seeing umpires in spray jackets with 'Fly Emirates' written across their backs and players with the golden arches of hamburger heaven as epaulettes on their once-white shirts. We have seen macho West Indians dressed in outfits the colour of strawberry mousse and an Australian team that makes it look as if the canaries are running the submarine. Purists have been offended so much that they have virtually apoplexed themselves into extinction. Is there, could there possibly be, a little corner of the mind or soul of a substantial minority that says, 'Bring back the flannelled

Addisons and the picket fences of yore'? Well, no, there isn't. We get the politicians and the cricketers we deserve. As a commentator once said, 'This is the current era we're living in.'

19

Memories of development

Within your 85 overs and my uncertain years
There's a moment of intersection, and it nears
Eyes and hands only, all else subordinate
I speed to our meeting.

from *Deep Third Man Addresses the Ball*, Amy Witting

'What was it like for you, the first time? Was it all over in a couple of minutes?' a friend once asked.

'Certainly not,' I told him, shocked. 'I stayed the whole day.'

The first time I saw test cricket was on 9 January 1959 at the Sydney Cricket Ground when England were 2–0 down in the 'throwing series'. There were 46 607 people there for the opening day of the third test, including actors John Mills and Trevor Howard among the cravats and binoculars in the Members' Stand, and Peter May's fiancée Virginia Gilligan, daughter of former England captain, 'What do you think, Arthur?' Gilligan. A school friend and I sat in the Bob Stand opposite and saw the match-winners from the second test, Alan Davidson and Ian Meckiff, take the new ball. They were the first pair of left-arm pace bowlers to open the Australian attack and they made an impact on many levels. This was test cricket, the real thing, and it was only later that I discovered other forms of international competition, on the high seas and under the Alps.

Davo was something of a cult figure at the time, so much so that a publican in Flinders Street near the ground advertised his yellow-tiler in big neon signs as 'Alan Davidson's Palace Hotel'. It was a crock of the first magnitude; the fine print above the door revealed the licensee to be one Alan P. Davidson, not the A.K. who had pioneered orthodoxy and wicket-taking for the left-arm pace fraternity, much as Rod Laver had given a backhand and dignity to the southpaws of tennis. Davo bowled just like a right-hander, and indeed that's what he looked like in the mirrors of the SCG bars.

Alan Keith Davidson had the classic fifteen-pace run-up and coiled spring delivery that Harold Larwood and Ray Lindwall had before him, while Meckiff was very much the Voce figure. He looked more like a golfer than a cricketer, so it was a bit of a surprise when he began his slow and awkward run, at the end of which he suddenly hurled the ball at the batsman as if to say, 'Oh here, have the bloody thing, and I hope it bites you!' It was impossible to tell if he threw the ball without a microscopic view of his jerky, angular delivery and its results; the 'Meckiff's a chucker' controversy was largely confined to the press box and no one in the crowd even called out 'no ball!' Davidson was easier to read; he was all purpose and circular movement, with late outswing trawling like a well-baited fishhook, and his attitude to the batsman appeared quite different. He seemed to be saying, 'This is what a cricket ball looks like. I think you should know that.'

During the 'Lindmill' days, there was a similar duopoly, with the silky action of Lindwall providing a complete contrast to the short run and sudden, petulant sling of Keith Miller. You would think that cricketers all over the country would be imitating Lindwall, Larwood and Davidson rather than Miller, Meckiff and the big slinging Bill Voce, but you would be wrong.

It was the fashion then for young school players to imitate older school players who took their cue from test cricketers. When I was at my first school I loved tennis, hated golf, and felt ambivalent about cricket because I could never work out whether I should bat or bowl, and if the latter, what sort of action I should adopt. In the first XI, Dent and Lawrie were the Lindwall and Miller figures, with Dent being even more fluent and perfect in his action and Lawrie having even more of an 'I fling dung' demeanour.

Not every cricketer lived up to his image, of course. Davidson was praised for his immaculate length and was called 'the Claw' because of his fielding prowess. Meckiff was considered a wild card, an erratic bowler and no great shakes in the field. The third test in 1959 began with the defence-oriented Trevor 'Barnacle' Bailey going lbw to Meckiff, who then caught the other opener, Arthur Milton, off a Davidson full toss. Nevertheless, over the series and over the years, you would have to say that Davidson was a smooth man whereas Meckiff was hairy.

When I was shipped off to my second school, it was on the P&O liner *Oronsay* and the school was in Switzerland, where my engineer father had accepted a job with the World Health Organisation. At least in the meantime there was a kind of cricket, a series of deck-top matches with a rope ball played between the passengers and the crew or that oldest of staples, England v. Commonwealth. Constraints of space among the nets and lifeboats only allowed for a run-up of four paces, so I had to streamline everything and concentrate on the delivery stride. There was no room for imitations and I ended up with an action that enabled me to make the best use of what talents I had, including a modest element of pace that had never come with a longer approach. No longer smooth or hairy, I had five o'clock shadow and I was finally ready to play. Unfortunately the country I was headed for was not exactly the home of cricket.

Switzerland has many educational establishments, but the International School of Geneva is the best known, and it was there on a glorious spring day in early April that I found a musty cricket kit in a dungeon next to the *vestiaire*, as the changing rooms were called. I dragged it outside and began to unpack the stumps and pads, oblivious to the stares and shudders of the other students and the staff, some of whom were refugees from the sado-masochistic English class and sport system. There was no discipline or punishment as such at the school, just the frosty eye of the form mistress, Madame Briquet, who was like Raymond Chandler's description of Bogart: he could be tough without a gun.

Soon we were playing practice matches on sports afternoon with some pretty fair cricketers who came from Iran, Ceylon and other places on or near the Empire trail, including a spinner from Manly Boys' High called Stuart Romaine. One of the best was a Welsh student, Peter Grundy, who had fallen in with some Gauloise-smoking decadents in the Upper Sixth, some of whom were nineteen or twenty. The smell of linseed oil soon brought him back to the fold, however, and to the amazement of his friends he practised long and hard. They gave up on him and scooted off on their Lambrettas, probably to drink absinthe.

This kind of elitism was quite common at Ecolint, as the school was known, and there were lots of children of the Jet Set hanging about or forming hierarchies. Rita Hayworth's daughter Yasmin Khan was a twelve-year-old femme fatale, Hardy Kruger's daughter Christine was tall, blonde and unattainable ('the one who got away'), Cathy von Sternberg was the 'Blue Angel' of the coffee lounge, while the saturnine Michael Chaplin was as silent as his father's films. A beautiful Eurasian heiress with Indian and South American roots was part of this crop and I was fervently in love with her, so I was pleased when she sat down with a friend and an ice-cream to watch one of our games. Maybe I'll get to her through our shared Commonwealth heritage, I mused hopefully. In the event, I tripped, fell awkwardly, and was run out trying to retain the strike. Soon after Corie got up and left, her ice-cream finished. The next day she looked at me with a mixture of pity and disdain (60–40 for pity) in the big dark eyes and I realised I had the job ahead of me. There was no such thing as racism in the Jet Set, and there was no such thing as love, either. For a marriage merger, the female of this species would consider a doctor at the very least, and more likely a billionaire spiritual leader or a prince with a well-taxed principality. In the case of Corie, I rather fancied I could detect an innocence, a genuine person and soulmate under all the style, but it might have been just the eyes. On the few occasions when she looked at me I went partially deaf—which is not a good way to be when you are running between wickets.

With Peter Grundy on loan from the Gauloisie, the headmaster's son hitting them in the middle, a BP brat from Iran with sound technique and a good Canadian wicket-keeper, we were putting together a reasonable team. Feeling confident, and wanting to raise the school's profile, we issued a challenge to the Geneva Cricket Club, the expatriates' stronghold. They could not play us— fatally—until the last week of term, when most families had booked early holidays. In the case of Stuart Romaine, his parents had arranged a social occasion on that day. A social occasion! He added, quite unnecessarily, that he wasn't really Australian; he was born in England, spent just a few years in Manly and appeared to know more about Davos than Davo. In no way did he model himself on Gosford's finest, the man of fifteen paces.

We had a stylish Ceylonese opening bat, but he fell in with some beer-drinking reprobates who hung around the Cafe Movenpick and said he was giving up cricket. The good Canadian wicket-keeper had to attend several social occasions back in Toronto, but someone's Uzbekistanian cousin from Berlin would play, I was told. I put him at long-stop, where he was the busiest player on the field. As he didn't speak English, I relayed instructions through first slip, who spoke a bit of German. Unfortunately Peter Grundy's Trueman-derived run-up proved too long and he sprayed the new ball all over the place, so there were more than a few Teutonic oaths heard during that raw and gloomy afternoon. The headmaster came down to watch his son get a duck in one of many umpiring fiascos and the challenge of our young guns was turned aside. Stuart Romaine arrived in civvies towards the end and said it was a pity he wasn't able to turn out and provide some much-needed spin in the attack. The only bright spot was that Corie was not in the grandstand, where she would have been very much alone. Over a hamburger at the Cafe Movenpick (pronounced 'Mervyn Peake'), I reflected that things could not get much worse.

Although Ecolint v. Geneva had been a debacle, I was picked, in the summer of 1962, at the age of seventeen years and eleven months, to enter man's estate and represent Switzerland in 'international' one-day games against the British Armed Forces team from Paris. I pleaded briefly for Peter Grundy to be included, but I was the only student they wanted. Did I abandon my friends for the beer-swilling world of the international cricketer? Yes I did!

'What on earth is someone your age doing with all those wrinkles around your eyes?' asked the wife of one of the players and I mumbled something about 'days in the sun' as we assembled on a cool morning in late June. The oval where we played was in fact a circle, a general-purpose athletics field at the Gare des Eaux-Vives (station of waters-living) where we rolled the grass down and pegged out a coir mat. The Swiss looked at us with a mixture of pity and disdain (80/20 for disdain) as we warmed up, with Mont Blanc and associated alps forming a novel backdrop to the summer game. A light rail line ran along the northern end and when a train went past you would see all these pale faces giving out with a Swiss Stare (I'm convinced that's what they use to get holes in their cheese). For the average citizen of Geneva, this bizarre cricket business was further evidence of eccentric behaviour by 'les anglais' and proved that the sods must be crazy.

The English batsmen I had seen on that first day at the SCG in 1959 had included an overawed debutant called Ted Dexter, who made no contribution, the gentle persuader Colin Cowdrey, who coaxed the ball into gaps and probably sent flowers in the morning, and the punishment machine, Peter May. The precise and pointy-faced May had the best technique of any batsman I had ever seen, and his driving was straight and severe. He only made 42 that day, but they were surely 42 of the most ominous and sadistic runs ever made and his dismissal—brilliantly and courageously caught by Ken Mackay at point, diving straight at the bat—brought gasps of relief from the crowd. In retrospect, that was the moment when the Ashes began to look safe, but the collective subconscious noted it at the time.

The captain of the Switzerland team was the same age as May, had been to the same university (Cambridge) and probably went to Charterhouse, too; he certainly came from the same school of thought. Technically perfect when batting—and I envied the coaching he must have received—it turned out that was all he did. Like PM he didn't field as such and didn't even bowl at practice, but this was no act of hero-worship like my friend Grundy's borrowing of the long run-up of Freddy S. Trueman. It was an introduction to the English phenomenon of The Batsman Who Just Batted. Most Australians were all-rounders of some kind, like the great Davo himself, who batted ahead of the wicket-keeper and fielded at cover point, where he saved as many runs as he made. In his oddly titled book *A Game Enjoyed*, Peter May ascribed the loss of the 1958–59 test series to the fact that there were too many players in his team making their last tour on the big hard grounds of Australia (code for 'they fielded like statues').

I was young, hyperactive, and an amateur from a hot climate and I loved running about, 'foxing' balls and diving for catches, so they let me do it. I opened the bowling for Switzerland and was kept on for hours until

I had taken 3 for 85 with my consistent outswingers (they were consistent because I could not bowl an in-dipper). If there hadn't been so many dropped catches, mostly courtesy of the only other Australian in the team—genial, fortyish Dr Carter of Adelaide—then I would have taken about 7 for 35, but you can't alter international records.

One of my victims was Bill Frindall, then at the start of a tour of duty for NATO, and many years away from becoming the 'bearded wonder' of the BBC and their official scorer. He later wrote, 'I was bowled by a fellow called Buzo!' and I wondered why there was an exclamation mark. Dear me, Frinners! That's not very multicultural of you! Frindall complained—quite rightly—about the umpiring standards in Switzerland when he was run out after placing his bat in the 'Half-Moon Bay' area of a shrunken and stretched mat.

In this second match I was given out lbw to a ball that pitched about half a metre outside leg stump; news of the MCC's 1937 rule change had not yet arrived in Switzerland. It was only years later that FOCUS, the Swiss Federation Of Cricket Umpires and Scorers, put the game in that country on to a proper footing and a national competition with around sixteen teams (Berne, Royal Lankans etc.) got under way. It is a worldwide phenomenon that the standard of cricket in any country or area is determined first by the standard of the unglamorous arts of umpiring and scoring. Swiss FOCUS secretary Phil Gooda, a Queenslander, found that the players were not all that grateful:

> I'm still not certain why I drag myself away from home on the only day off that I get, travel about 100 miles, stand in either blazing heat or miserable drizzle, make on the spot decisions that affect at least 22 other people's weekends, often get angry faces and words directed at me, rarely get offered even a small beer afterwards and then reverse the process to get home to a quick snack and maybe, if I'm lucky, a half-hour or so with my Significant Other.

Those who played in the second match of the 1962 series would have bought you a pint, Phil!

We had a close win in the first match, lost the second (!), and then fronted for the third on a sparkling day in July. 'Don't drop it so short this time,' ordered The Batsman Who Just Batted and gave me the new ball. An hour later I had taken 5 for 6 against a disorganised, cat-on-hot-bricks opposition, bowling fuller and faster in the crisp air. The Armed Forces captain, who was in fact a major, spent a lot of time at the non-striker's end looking most displeased. 'Two of those wickits fell to eau verre pitched bawls,' I heard him say to the umpire. It was not unusual to converse with the umpire, but under this English code of behaviour there was not the slightest flicker of dissent, no matter how outrageous the decision.

That night in the gallery outside the Cafe Movenpick, Corie walked past, nodding vaguely at me. The sound of her echoing heels certainly brought the euphoric five-for-sixer back to earth. She had only seen me get run out at cricket and I hadn't done much more in class than name Noumea as the capital of New Caledonia, and I still wore desert boots. A vague nod is all you get for that.

We won the fourth and final 'test' easily, with my only contribution being an unexpected 32 with the bat, and then I got the news that I was being shipped home to sit for a 'post' to get into university. I wanted to stay on in Geneva and make some inroads with Corie but my exam results had not been spectacular and the parental hands were going on the hips. At the age of eighteen my Indian summer was over.

Reality struck when I fronted up to the wizened coach of North Sydney on a baking day in late October. He was called Jimmy Hannan, as indeed a lot of people were in those days, and I asked him if I could join the club. 'Where've you been playing?' he asked. 'I've just represented Switzerland,' I answered, aiming for a note of objectivity. He looked at me with a mixture of disgust and disdain (95–5 for disgust) and said 'Switzerland! Not exactly the home of cricket, is it?' I spent that season, 1962–63, playing for North Sydney Colts as a batsman (top score: 33) while Europe froze in the coldest winter of the twentieth century. The voyage of identity and image, if that's what it was, had well and truly ended. For a clincher, Davo had added an in-dipper to his consummate 'follow me boys' outswinger and put himself beyond the reach of imitation, let alone emulation.

What happened to Corie? Reader, she married a doctor and they play lots of golf.

Note: Alan Davidson retired at the end of the 1962–63 season.

20

The 1942 Ashes tour

I may have been blinded by the glitter and pomp of my first trip to England in that summer of 1921, but it seemed to me that servants had a fine respect for their masters and there existed a reciprocity which brought a full measure of happiness and understanding into the life of the average Englishman. Farm hands were not very well paid perhaps, in relation to their wealthy employers, but they seemed to be happy and well attuned to the real and wholesome things of life.

from *10 for 66 and All That*, Arthur Mailey

The newspapers blew across the empty field. There was no Warwick Armstrong to pick one up and read it. The air raid siren had sounded and the streets were deserted, leaving only the smell of pies baking in Lyons Corner

House and the hum of a dozen Messerschmitts. This was England in 1942. There were plenty who said the cricket should not go ahead as there was a war on, but Winston Churchill made a Solomon-like decision. Let the Australians come, he decreed, but go easy on the publicity. Let life go on, but we should not get carried away and waste our time on frivolous pursuits. It is, after all, only a game.

Piecing together what happened on that 1942 tour has been difficult for cricket historians, and most have pretended that it simply did not take place. What we do know is that under the enlightened captaincy of Don Bradman and Wally Hammond there was sportsmanship, good behaviour and a fine spirit of reciprocity between the teams that was exemplified when the Don took the boys to see Gloucestershire playing at Lord's. The 39-year-old Wally was in the process of making one of his elegant, powerful but almost certainly autumnal centuries and the Don turned to the bar where some of his players were drinking beer. 'Come and have a look at this, you fellows,' he said, 'You may never see its like again.' Later that day Wally and the Don were sipping lemonade in the Long Room, when the Australian skipper noticed something different.

'Where are the portraits of Lord Harris and Lord Hawke?' he asked the MCC Secretary.

'We took them down,' was the reply. 'We found irrefutable proof that they had drawn up the schedules for the 1921 and 1926 Ashes tours with a view to tiring out the Aussies and programming the most distant games—Glamorgan, Lancashire, Sussex, as the case may be—before test matches. It was disgraceful. Both of those bounders are dead, and I'll be damned if I want their ugly mugs looking down at me. By the way, Don, here are the Ashes. You won them fair and square in '34. They'll only come back here when we win a series.'

The Old Trafford test began in controversy when the start of play was delayed for some hours as the ground staff beavered away on the pitch. There was no announcement, of course, and the spectators had to work out what happened as best they could. Announcements! Pshaw! If you don't know what's going on, then that's your lookout, chum. What transpired was that Wally approached the Don on the morning of the match and said the groundsman had just been sacked for preparing a pitch that unduly favoured England's off-spinners.

'But we have an offie in our team, Wally,' countered the Don, 'You know Ian Johnson.'

'Yes, and a fine player he is, too. You don't need a crystal ball to work out that he'll captain Australia one day and lead by example. But Johnno's a flight bowler, Don. He's beaten me through the air more times than I care to recall. This wicket has been prepared for those who give it a bit more of a tweak, like our own Hedley Verity. Heds may be a Yorkshireman, and the Wars of the Roses not long over, but this OT wicket has been unfairly tailored for him.'

'But what about the groundsman's wife and children? Will they be provided for?'

'He should have thought of that before, Don. As it turns out, he never married.'

'So he never . . . ?'

'Occupied the crease? Apparently not.'

'I think I know who'll be most upset that this doctoring was even thought of . . . '

'Hedley Verity.'

'It's a no-brainer.'

No actual record exists of this conversation between the Boy from Bowral and the Cirencester Kid, but it was put together by a committee of Melbourne playwrights working from available evidence. When a groundsman was sacked on the morning of the Leeds test, we do know that Bradman inquired about the reason and was told that the fellow had been loafing. Walter Hammond's statement is on the record: 'There were two groundsmen out there, but only one of them was preparing a wicket.'

After a spirited draw at Trent Bridge ('A fine start to the series, Don,' said a beaming Wally) the teams went to Lord's, where the MCC Secretary apologised to the

Australians about the ridge in the pitch: 'We'll get it fixed as soon as we can, but there's a war on, you know.'

'I know,' said the Don sympathetically as he watched Bill Brown walk after getting a tickle to the keeper.

'A cup of tea, sir?' inquired a smiling WAAC, but Braddles had to decline.

'I'd love one,' he said, 'but I have to go and bat. Excuse me.'

'There's just one more thing.'

'What is it?'

'Best of luck, sir,' declared the WAAC with shining eyes.

When Don was on 254 Wally waved back the twelfth man with drinks and later upbraided him. 'You don't bring on drinks when a man's about to break his record score at this ground,' said the skipper.

'Sorry, Wally,' mumbled the twelfthy, 'but there was no announcement.'

'What the Dickens would be the use of that? You can read the scoreboard, can't you?'

'Yes, Wally.'

'The whole idea of this wonderful game is that you have to decode things for yourself. If we ever had ground announcers . . . well, you might as well go to Luna Park. It just wouldn't be cricket.'

On a golden summer's day at Fenner's, before death duties, immigration and property development had the land lying fallow and the fish floating belly-up in the Cam, Australia lost narrowly to Cambridge University and the Don had to answer charges that he had Maliked the situation. 'We were simply outplayed,' he countered. 'Full credit to the Cambridge boys for their gutsy effort.'

In the Leeds test, Bradman made 502 and was congratulated on his world record score by Wally and his team. 'I want it expunged from the scorebooks,' said the Don later. 'England were a bowler short and that track was a shirtfront. Besides, there's more to cricket than just piling up big scores.'

These are some of the problems the cricket historian is tempted to call insuperable. The series was played in such good spirit that most of the records have been lost or deliberately destroyed in the name of sportsmanship. We know for example that Len Hutton made a pair at the Oval in the fifth test, but is it true that he said to Bill O'Reilly, 'I hope this makes up for all those runs I took off you in 1938'? There is also the wartime security aspect. In a Cairo bar on the way over to England Don Bradman was approached by a bookmaker called John and a monocled expat called Erich. 'What's it worth to you to lose the Ashes?' asked John.

The Don replied, 'What Ashes? I'm going to join up.'

'I vould like to see your schedule, and I vill pay good money for zis document,' ventured Erich.

'Get back to Krautland,' was the Boy from Bowral's response. 'We don't want your type here. Maestro! Do you know the *Marseillaise*?'

And the band played on, just as Don did to Eric Hollies in 1948.

Author's biography

RALPH HENDERSON

AB was born in Sydney and educated at the University of NSW, where he played for the 3rd XI, earned a BA, and won the Alumni Award in 1998 for his contribution to Australian literature.

His humorous and original books include *Tautology*, *Prue Flies North*, *Kiwese*, *Pacific Union* and *A Dictionary of the Almost Obvious*. With Jamie Grant he co-edited *The Longest Game*, a unique collection of cricket writing.